Methods and Methodologies in Heritage Studies

Methods and Methodologies in Heritage Studies

Edited by

Rachel King and Trinidad Rico

UCL Press, the UK's first fully open access university press, has established a new open access textbook programme. Publishing for courses and modules both at UCL and for use at universities globally, it reflects our commitment to widening the use of open educational resources. The rising cost of textbooks, combined with issues of availability, particularly digitally, are a challenge for universities and a potential barrier to student learning. The textbooks in this programme provide benefits to students by removing those barriers and have been commissioned and developed with student use in mind. Open access publishing provides a means to make textbooks accessible to a wider audience, while also reducing the burden on library budgets.

If you are using this textbook to teach a course at your institution, please notify us at uclpresspublishing@ucl.ac.uk so that we can track adoptions and build metrics that evidence how open access textbooks are used and the value they deliver. We welcome your feedback on this book and the programme, do get in touch to tell us your thoughts.

First published in 2024 by
UCL Press
University College London
Gower Street
London WC1E 6BT

Available to download free: www.uclpress.co.uk

A CIP catalogue record for this book is available from The British Library.

ISBN: 978-1-80008-381-3 (Hbk.)
ISBN: 978-1-80008-380-6 (Pbk.)
ISBN: 978-1-80008-379-0 (PDF)
ISBN: 978-1-80008-382-0 (epub)
DOI: https://doi.org/10.14324/111.9781800083790

CONTENTS

LIST OF CONTRIBUTORS

Melissa F. Baird
Department of Social Sciences
Michigan Technological University, USA

David Francis
Department of Culture, Media and Creative Industries
Kings College London, UK

Ömür Harmanşah
School of Art & Art History
University of Illinois Chicago, USA

Rachel King
UCL Institute of Archaeology
University College London, UK

Christina Luke
Archaeology and History of Art
Koç University, Turkey

Tebogo George Mahashe
Michaelis School of Fine Art
University of Cape Town, South Africa

Elizabeth Marlowe
Museum Studies and Department of Art
Colgate University, USA

Laura McAtackney
Department of Archaeology and Heritage Studies
Aarhus Universitet, Denmark

Colleen Morgan
Department of Archaeology
University of York, UK

María de los Ángeles Picone
Department of History
Boston College, USA

Trinidad Rico
Cultural Heritage and Preservation Studies,
Department of Art History
Rutgers University, USA

Uzma Z. Rizvi
Department of Social Science and Cultural Studies
Pratt Institute, USA

Colin Sterling
Department of Arts and Culture
University of Amsterdam, The Netherlands

Alice Stevenson
UCL Institute of Archaeology
University College London, UK

Victoria Vargas-Downing
School of Fine Art, History of Art and Cultural Studies
University of Leeds, UK

Yujie Zhu
ANU Centre for Heritage and Museum Studies
The Australian National University, Australia

Leticia Zuppardi
Facultad de Información y Comunicación
Universidad de la República, Uruguay

1 Introduction: epistemic journeys

Trinidad Rico and Rachel King

WHY HERITAGE METHODS?

There is a crisis of identity in the field of heritage studies. While the study of heritage continues to gain traction in graduate and undergraduate programmes across the world, the path to studying heritage value is somewhat elusive. Some scholars and practitioners have been trained in archaeology, anthropology or even sociology departments. Others come from architecture programmes, public history programmes, folklore, museum studies, art history, chemistry ... the list goes on. This extreme trans-disciplinarity is as promising as it is problematic. There is hardly a canon for the study of heritage and its preservation, and the lack of single-track disciplinary training in this field has made the idea of a shared set of methods unfeasible. The question of **methods** – intellectual tools for gathering evidence and shaping knowledge about heritage – is rarely addressed specifically in relevant scholarship or in educational curricula.

This is a book about making knowledge in heritage studies; specifically, it considers how we understand heritage value through diverse, usually qualitative, sources. Foremost, it is a compilation of intellectual journeys focused on **epistemology**: the processes through which data are created, transformed into evidence, assembled into conclusions and validated within a knowledge community. This volume brings together different scholars who summarise distinct epistemic journeys in the field that result in diverse understandings of heritage.

Broadly speaking, ideas about the value of the past in the present have long been dominated by a preservationist episteme: a way of thinking about the past that privileges physical endurance, the notion that one-of-a-kind uniqueness is evidence of significance and a strong attachment to specific periods in history. This prevailing wisdom, inherited from older art historical and antiquarian paradigms, dictated that a site or a structure that could weather the passing of time and conform to particular aesthetic standards had proven its significance and worth. As institutions like UNESCO internationalised heritage value in the years following World War II, this dominant heritage discourse consolidated and promoted universalised ideals of heritage as an avenue for international consensus and peacebuilding.

This mode of thinking and governing heritage led to a **methodology** – a package of methods for gathering data – rooted in a specific rationale that may be familiar because it has endured for so long: recording and preserving elements of the past primarily through text (e.g. policy) and image (e.g. documentation). Heritage value was thus accessible through historical representations in archives and photographs. Accessing and interpreting this value, though, required certain disciplinary training and expertise. Therefore, the ways in which heritage is imagined, the methodological toolkits perfected to access them and the disciplinary training in the emerging field of heritage studies and preservation are all contained within each other in a tautological loop: for example, visual documentation of a heritage site will only ever produce visual data, reaffirming its visual properties, and so on. With limited alterations in their goals, visual methods (in particular) endured as the core of this field of study, going from artistic, and then architectural, records of heritage places to three-dimensional scanning of complex surfaces and volumes (Brusius and Rico 2023). Advances in scientific precision for these methods did little to change the scope and scale of the data that visual methods could obtain, despite the fact that disciplinary ideas of heritage value began to distance themselves from visuality, as we describe later in this chapter. Every method has its limitations.

During the 1980s, the remit of heritage studies shifted from an exclusive focus on material culture to a more sophisticated turn towards heritage *subjects*. That is, it became a field 'concerned first and foremost with people, shaped by a diverse range of social practices, processes and experiences' (Filippucci 2009, 320).

Heritage, in this context, came to be seen through an episteme that we can loosely call constructivism: heritage in this sense is not ready-made in the world but rather something that is produced through rhetoric (Lafrenz Samuels and Rico 2015), contingent on diverse actors and values. This episteme included a reflexive awareness of the ways in which heritage as a field was part of an influential ecosystem of *heritage making*. While early interventions focused on how this ecosystem functioned as a particularly nationalist industry (Hewison 1987), subsequent thinking expanded globally through documenting how heritage helps to assemble networks of influence across territories, institutions and scales (Meskell 2015).

Such a shift in thinking means that the study of heritage has set itself the task of mapping the complexities of the past, but also of tracking colonial legacies, local realities, changing actors and overlapping ideologies. Moreover, a field that has turned its attention to the problem of historical and contemporary invisibility and exclusion is increasingly aware of the dangerous ways in which heritage preservation itself has been a force of erasure and marginalisation. There is a methodological consideration in this critical self-awareness; that is, acknowledging where the narrow gaze produced by certain methodological toolkits has excluded essential qualities and voices in heritage narratives. These omitted perspectives are now alienated from the institutions and forms of knowledge that guard heritage value in the name of humanity. Studying heritage from a more reflexive perspective is therefore not the same as safeguarding or preserving it, but both endeavours benefit extraordinarily from these critical views in order to understand their own shortcomings and avoid supporting the injustices they created.

Such a dramatic expansion of concerns with diversity and inclusion in heritage representations allowed two redirections. The first emphasised an increasing sensitivity to practices of marginalisation, exclusion and erasure, manifested in the foregrounding of *politics* as a key interpretive lens for the work of heritage and preservation. Second, the gradual inclusion of underrepresented experiences in the corpus of knowledge associated with heritage value resulted in an explosion of meaning for heritage in general: living and cultural landscapes, intangible heritage, performances, spirituality, and more. Many forms of knowledge that inform and capture these experiences have since become the 'new normal' for this field, inviting consideration of other experiential dimensions that construct and sustain heritage value outside of the visual and historical regime.

Therefore, the growth of a theoretical backbone for heritage studies that responds to these concerns – what some have called the 'critical turn' – called for a reality check (Winter 2013). How and with what evidence are we making knowledge about heritage? The long history of traditional preservationist methods in heritage studies and practices suggests that perhaps the largest hurdle for the field is disarming its own teleology; that is, the way in which its approaches have derived from and been propelled by a limited set of ideas. Put differently, paying attention to how methodologies work to make knowledge about heritage shows us where our habits of reason and research have led us as a community of practitioners – and where we may need to intervene. This volume proposes such an intervention. It results from our own epistemic journeys through both doing and teaching heritage and preservation. In putting together this volume, we respond to Lynn Meskell's (2015, 3) call for a heritage scholarship that is disciplinarily grounded and attached to methodological and intellectual commitments. Without these, studies of heritage tend towards the descriptive and momentary, relying more on modes of representation than on the results of committed and ethical analysis.

WHAT DO WE MEAN BY HERITAGE VALUE AND ITS METHODOLOGIES?

The agnosticism about the intellectual roots of heritage research that Meskell warns against is partly a legacy of the discursive turn within critical heritage studies, which broadly considered how ideas about heritage value are produced socially and institutionally (see Chapters 9 and 13). The rapid expansion of heritage discourse as an area of theoretical intervention, along with its cross- and interdisciplinary practices and interests, has made it more important than ever to be explicit about the epistemologies in question – how specific conceptualisations of heritage are linked with relevant methodologies. The idea of 'journeys' that we use here indicates precisely how heritage studies grew in conversation with other disciplinary traditions, enabling intellectual itineraries that have affected heritage studies at different points in its relatively short history.

What do we mean, then, by epistemology in practice? And where does empiricism reside in the study of heritage? A partial answer to this is found in methodologies, and here it is useful to clarify how we distinguish these from methods. The production and use of case studies is a useful methodology to illustrate this. Fundamentally, a case study aims to use an in-depth examination of a particular contextualised situation or phenomenon to understand something broader and more widely applicable about a concept or issue. Within a case study, a researcher can use a number of methods to analyse their subject: for example, archival analysis (Chapter 5) can be used to establish the historical circumstances of the case, and discourse analysis (Chapter 13) helps to dissect how ideas circulate and are negotiated among relevant people and institutions. Methodology is thus a research design and rationale, while methods are techniques that respond to the aims and promises of the research question with the explicit purpose of producing data. When we stated earlier that an over-reliance on case studies within heritage scholarship has resulted in a weak attention to methodological detail, we mean that the methods making up case studies and how these produce distinct kinds of empirical evidence are often overlooked or deemed so obvious as to make critical description unnecessary.

Another way of maintaining empiricism is to be clear about what it is we are studying and documenting. It is never enough to claim to study 'heritage' because, as we have described, scholarly turns in heritage studies since the 1990s have established that this is subjective, complex and varied in character. These same turns have highlighted how committing to centre agency and actors in our work ultimately compels an analytical focus on *heritage value*, that is, a quality bestowed on something by someone. Here is where the examination of how knowledge is made becomes essential, not just for the production of sound research but also for subjecting heritage studies as a field to careful scrutiny. In one of the first volumes tackling heritage methods, Sørensen and Carman (2009, 3) motivated readers to 'make the means transparent', dividing methods in heritage studies into three broad categories: discursive (about words), behavioural (about attitudes) and qualitative (about dimensions) – a trilogy of 'text', 'people' and 'object' that recognised the expanding interdisciplinarity that the field was experiencing already. But even these categories impose inherited dimensions to the study of heritage value that are attached to colonial and authoritative structures carried over by their original disciplinary stewards. The centralisation of 'alternative' values and knowledge systems by once-marginal stakeholders requires a complete epistemological decolonisation (Tuhiwai Smith 2021, 239). At heart, this recognises that methods and methodologies themselves alter, rather than simply capture, the conditions of heritage value.

It is important to consider that throughout most of its disciplinary history, heritage was considered an inalienable value that required little justification. As an example, the entire bilingual advisory evaluation of the Taj Mahal for inclusion in UNESCO's World Heritage List in 1982 has a total of three pages and starts with identifying the mausoleum as 'one of the most famous monuments in the world'. In contrast, the three properties successfully inscribed on the same list in 2023 are accompanied by advisory evaluations that span 25, 12, and 38 pages respectively, for the English-language version alone. This shift illustrates how, over time, heritage value has required significantly more contextualisation and comparison in order to be recognised by a global community of experts and maintain a myth of uniqueness.

The origins of heritage as a self-evident and intrinsic characteristic also meant that the core of methodologies for studying heritage revolved around capturing factors *affecting* heritage: mechanical, chemical and other environmental and social forces affecting the integrity and authenticity of heritage places and things. The documentation of risk factors, threats and related destruction has been a defining feature of the historiography of heritage and preservation studies. Reflecting these concerns, modes of documentation have evolved, one could say, from capturing heritage in simple drawings and photography to 3D scanning and remote sensing, archiving and circulating heritage value as an aesthetic, measurable and tangible quality with different levels of precision. The reality is more complex.

By accepting that heritage value is always contingent and always in-the-making, constructivist epistemes have called upon a wider range of both methodologies and methods that respond to the conditions in which heritage value exists and the sources in which it resides. With an embrace of fluidity came an embrace of movement, both chronological and spatial. New approaches emerged at an intersection between the spatial sciences and social sciences to understand heritage value as it is constituted and maintained through itineraries and travel – of people, ideas and politics (Graves-Brown and Schofield 2019; Holley-Kline and Papazian 2020). Aligned with the critical turn and heavily influenced by developments in archaeology, a growing attention to political forces that shape heritage narratives prompted a turn to participatory methods and expertise. We can recognise these both as a package of knowledge and techniques as well as the spheres of influence and standards of institutional and bureaucratic traditions that create the macro structure of heritage meaning (Chapter 9). With newfound interest in identifying, supporting and anticipating marginalised viewpoints, the heritage and preservation field looked to anthropological methods, that is, close-to-the-ground methods that allow us to observe lived experiences and heritage making in real time (Chapter 15).

At the same time, a different claim to improve access to heritage interpretation and management has come to define heritage studies in the twenty-first century: innovations in digital technologies and methodologies have similarly promised more accessible, socially nuanced approaches to heritage (Bonacchi 2022). The digital turn has proposed to increase access and democratisation to heritage decision-making through digital archiving, crowdsourcing and technologically sophisticated forms of representing heritage resources and stakeholder claims.

The allure of technology as a tool for decolonisation has been particularly noticeable in claims to improve access for marginalised groups and in the promise to deliver heritage safeguarding, particularly prominent among advocates of 3D scanning over the last few decades. Such technocratic aspirations and its rhetoric have origins in the earliest days of global heritage preservationism and, we now know, can distance heritage value from the political and social contexts in which it operates (Rico 2017; Meskell 2018), aligning instead with the scientific rigidity that many of the methods (and ethics) in this volume challenge. But 'digital heritage' has also had a positive impact on the critical turn in heritage studies (Chapter 18): questions of storage and accessibility, digital publics and literacy, and the use of qualitative and quantitative datasets constitute the line separating, on the one hand, a digital turn that grows in dialogue with heritage ethics and, on the other hand, a technocratic field that evolves away from the concerns of the critical turn – in the latter, heritage is simply a platform for the development of techniques (see Jones et al. 2018; Gupta et al. 2020; Bonacchi 2022; Morgan 2022 for discussion).

More recently, heritage studies has also reassessed its relationship to visual studies. As we discussed in this introduction, throughout its history the study and management of heritage has relied extensively on unproblematised visual languages and archives while, at the same time, it distanced itself from older art historical paradigms during the critical turn. This resulted in a weak attention to the politics of representation at the core of the critical turn (Chapter 3). A more recent reassessment of the use and circulation of images incorporated key debates and methods from art history and the history of science to challenge the field's heavy and uncritical reliance on visuality. These interventions, for example, examine the contemporary production of images of iconoclasm and its uses as empirical evidence (Harmanşah 2015), and confront the relationships between visual archives, practices of acquisition and representation, and stewardship (Brusius and Rico 2023). These scholars have asked that we carefully reconsider the conditions and intentions surrounding the production and the producers of these images before we disseminate them as representative of objective heritage narratives. In this way, the epistemic journey in the study of heritage has come full circle, revisiting the very foundational orientations of the field – capturing 'history' in predominantly visual media – now with a mature rejection of the claims of objectivity that many of the original founders of the field claimed to achieve.

HOW TO READ AND USE THIS BOOK

With all this in mind and by taking *heritage value* as our focus, this volume supports a specific argument. Namely, that any discussion of methodology has to contend with varied intellectual histories of technology, politics (global, local and everything in between), preoccupations with loss, ethical transgressions and decolonial aspirations. This realisation asks us to treat interdisciplinarity creatively and carefully, with special attention to the trajectories of particular methods and research problems and how these have been expressed in practice. Our book sections reflect this. Nine chapters offer discussions on key areas in which heritage value is negotiated, summarised and critiqued by experts in the field: documents, archives, collections, institutions, landscapes, discourses, practices, publics and training. Interspersed between chapters are short contributions that invite a discussion to be taken 'out of the box'. These are interventions, clarifications and expansions of arguments in this book that enlarge our understanding of heritage value. These not only connect arguments to each other but also connect the field to other disciplinary approaches and concerns yet to be explored. Readers are invited to take note of the diversity of disciplinary languages, training and experience of our contributors and how this is reflected in the voices featured throughout these contributions.

Everything we think we know about heritage value, how it is constructed, circulated and consumed, as well as the good and the bad impact of our work, can change. Readers will learn that throughout the historiography of heritage studies, ideas of value, stewardship and access have transformed dramatically in alignment with the changing context of conservation and the politics of cultural debates at local and global scales. Heritage, once considered a value that could be observed at the surface level, has been revealed to exist mostly underground (Byrne 2007). How we search for the invisible that is also hiding in plain sight is one of the major unresolved challenges of this field. In the final chapter of this volume, we expand on how we see this and other open questions related to the future of teaching and training in heritage studies.

In foregrounding epistemology in these intellectual contexts, this volume also encourages us to expand 'the palate of heritage theory' (Tolia-Kelly et al. 2016, 1; cf. Waterton and Watson 2013). Therefore, in addition to understanding how to go about assembling heritage research (particularly at the nexus of archaeology, anthropology, history, art history and geography), we also hope that readers use this book to become confident *users* of heritage research. By this we are referring to a form of research literacy in heritage studies, whereby anyone with a critical interest in heritage can interrogate data and trace epistemic journeys with confidence as a student, scholar, manager, policymaker, funder or activist.

Accordingly, this is not a handbook of heritage *topics*. Nor it is an encyclopaedia that captures every method or data source that can contribute to the study of heritage value. Such a project would be doomed from the start, considering the rate at which the field is growing. This book is also not meant to be an operational handbook – providing instructions for how to carry out a specific piece of work – although we certainly hope the ideas presented here will help inform those decisions. Instead, the contributors in this volume address key contemporary challenges in the study and preservation of heritage value through different research strategies, questions and scales of analysis. At the same time, we caution against favouring any one approach over others. None of these approaches can serve as the sole answer to the methodological problems of heritage studies. As the contributors to this volume demonstrate, there are multiple methodologies available for interrogating heritage value, as long as we pay attention to the specifics of how they work. In the following section – 'On connecting' – we offer some suggestions for how to approach the work of assembling these methodologies.

ACKNOWLEDGEMENTS

This volume was conceptualised in 2018 in the grounds of UCL's Institute of Archaeology and intended to be concretised at the Association for Critical Heritage Studies biannual conference in London during the early months of the COVID-19 pandemic. Its contributors endured academic transitions, career breaks, a devastating earthquake (Turkey) and different health challenges. Because of this, we are eternally grateful to the colleagues who committed to this project with patience and generosity and to the supportive reviewers and editors for their encouragement.

REFERENCES AND RESOURCES

Bonacchi, Chiara. 2022. *Heritage and Nationalism: Understanding populism through big data*. London: UCL Press.

Brusius, Mirjam and Trinidad Rico. 2023. 'Counter-archives as heritage justice: Photography, invisible labor and peopled ruins'. *Journal of Visual Culture* 21(3): 64–92.

Byrne, Denis. 2007. *Surface Collection: Archaeological travels in Southeast Asia*. Lanham, MD: AltaMira Press.

Filippucci, Paula. 2009. 'Heritage and methodology: A view from social anthropology'. In *Heritage Studies: Methods and approaches*, edited by Marie Louise Stig Sørensen and John Carman, 319 25. London: Routledge.

Graves-Brown, Paul and John Schofield. 2019. 'Encountering landscape: Travel as method'. *Landscapes* 20(1): 61–84.

Gupta, Neha, Sue Blair and Ramona Nicholas. 2020. 'What we see, what we don't see: Data governance, archaeological spatial databases and the rights of indigenous peoples in an age of big data'. *Journal of Field Archaeology* 45(sup. 1): S39–S50.

Harmanşah, Ömür. 2015. 'ISIS, heritage, and the spectacles of destruction in the global media'. *Near Eastern Archaeology* 78(3): 170–7.

Hewison, Robert. 1987. *The Heritage Industry: Britain in a climate of decline*. London: Methuen.

Holley-Kline, Sam and Sabrina Papazian. 2020. 'Heritage trekking: Toward an integrated heritage studies methodology'. *Journal of Field Archaeology* 45(7): 527–41.

ICOMOS. 1983. 'Advisory Body evaluation (ICOMOS) / Évaluation de l'organisation consultative (ICOMOS)'. Accessed 14 March 2024. https://whc.unesco.org/en/list/252/documents/.

Jones, Siân, Stuart Jeffrey, Mhairi Maxwell, Alex Hale and Cara Jones. 2018. '3D heritage visualisation and the negotiation of authenticity: The ACCORD project'. *International Journal of Heritage Studies* 24(4): 333–53.

Lafrenz Samuels, Kathryn and Trinidad Rico. 2015. *Heritage Keywords: Rhetoric and redescription in cultural heritage*. Boulder, CO: University Press of Colorado.

Meskell, Lynn. 2015. 'Introduction: Globalizing heritage'. In *Global Heritage: A reader*, edited by Lynn Meskell, 1–21. Hoboken, NJ: Wiley-Blackwell.

Meskell, Lynn. 2018. *A Future in Ruins: UNESCO, world heritage, and the dream of peace*. Oxford: Oxford University Press.

Morgan, Colleen. 2022. 'Current digital archaeology'. *Annual Review of Anthropology* 51: 213–31.

Rico, Trinidad. 2017. 'Technology, technocracy, and the promise of "alternative" heritage values'. In *Heritage in Action*, edited by Helaine Silverman, Emma Waterton and Steve Watson, 217–30. New York: Springer Press.

Smith, Linda Tuhiwai. 2021. *Decolonizing Methodologies: Research and Indigenous peoples*. 3rd ed. London: Zed Books.

Sørensen, Marie Louise Stig and John Carman (eds) 2009. 'Introduction: Making the means transparent: Reasons and reflections'. In *Heritage Studies: Methods and approaches*, edited by Marie Louise Stig Sørensen and John Carman, 1–10. London: Routledge.

Tolia-Kelly, Divya P., Emma Waterton and Steve Watson. 2016. 'Introduction: Heritage, affect and emotion'. In *Heritage, Affect and Emotion*, edited by Divya P. Tolia-Kelly, Emma Waterton and Steve Watson, 1–11. London: Routledge.

Waterton, Emma and Steve Watson. 2013. 'Framing theory: Towards a critical imagination in heritage studies'. *International Journal of Heritage Studies* 19(6): 546–61.

Winter, Tim. 2013. 'Clarifying the critical in critical heritage studies'. *International Journal of Heritage Studies* 19(6): 532–45.

2 On connecting

Rachel King and Trinidad Rico

In this volume we propose a problem-oriented approach: each chapter reflects a major topic, source material or unit of analysis that, taken together, represent the core issues that students and teachers will encounter in studying how heritage values are shaped. Each chapter includes disciplinary histories of its subject matter that trace the epistemic journeys and intellectual machineries that propel methodologies forward. Contributors are explicit about where methods are located in relation to the generation of specific heritage values. They describe when methods can be activated, what sources of data they are able to deal with, and what limitations need to be considered. For this purpose, each chapter follows a uniform structure that allows the volume to function as a handbook that can be utilised in support of a variety of courses:

- *Description and historiography*: How and when did the study of heritage value engage with the chapter's subject? This section addresses methodological approaches within the subject's ideological context and trajectory.
- *Praxis*: This section puts methods and methodologies in context.
- *Teaching*: How does one train people on the productive, correct and ethical use of the approach identified? This section identifies the pedagogy and practice that an author believes most effectively transmits this approach to students in higher education or practice-based contexts.
- *References and resources*: In addition to a list of works cited, contributors provide other key readings and resources that they would recommend in order to expand upon chapter discussions and implement different approaches.

A second type of contribution in this volume is short discussions that identify further challenges, counter-arguments and cutting-edge approaches from adjacent disciplines. These support the project of refining heritage methods and methodologies while also paving the way for the next generation of methods. Many of these contributors and their approaches operate outside of heritage studies altogether but have much to offer to our understanding of epistemology in this field. These contributions may also offer resources and further reading to support a familiarity with these approaches.

With the diversity of contributions offered, there are two ways to use this volume for teaching and learning. One is to read it in the order in which chapters are arranged, organised roughly chronologically from older and more established approaches to newer challenges. This sequence reflects the ways in which heritage methods and methodologies were concerned, initially, with the more concrete qualities of heritage value (e.g. aesthetics) supported by the canon of established disciplines (e.g. art history). The volume then curates more intangible and fluid ways of thinking about the qualities and locations of heritage value that often transcend disciplinary boundaries (e.g. discourse).

A second way of using this volume is to approach it with a specific interest in mind and use the various chapters to assemble a methodological package that responds to a research question – to chart a user's own epistemic journey. For example, approaches could be ordered from those more suited to the study of global heritage to those supporting a more localised approach. This sort of 'hopscotch' is possible thanks to the ways in which authors themselves connect topics and keywords across the book and facilitated using hyperlinks in the online format of this volume. A few examples of these connections across the volume are in Table 2.1.

Finally, readers are encouraged to consider how the layout of chapters in this volume, the themes selected for inclusion, the regions of the world represented in its chapters, the authors curated and the disciplinary training that each of its contributors brings to the conversation give shape to specific ideas of heritage value.

Table 2.1 Connections between topics and keywords across the book

Topic	Stop 1	Stop 2	Stop 3	Stop 4
Intangible heritage	Practices and performances	On locality	*Meloro*: on dreaming	On speaking
Grassroots heritage	Institutions and governance	On locality	Practices and performances	Evaluation and publics
Official heritage	Discourses and languages	Institutions and governance	Documents and records	Collections and collecting
Heritage and memory	Archives and historiography	On commemorating	*Meloro*: on dreaming	Practices and performances
Heritage and nationalism	Collections and collecting	Institutions and governance	On borderlands	Archives and historiography
Heritage networks	Discourses and languages	Institutions and governance	Collections and collecting	On digital connection
Heritage tourism	On locality	Landscapes and environment	Evaluation and publics	Discourses and languages
Heritage and space	Landscapes and environment	On borderlands	On commemorating	Institutions and governance

3 Documents and records

Colin Sterling

DESCRIPTION AND HISTORIOGRAPHY

> *Modern memory is, above all, archival. It relies entirely on the materiality of the trace, the immediacy of the recording, the visibility of the image. (Nora 1989, 13)*

How and why certain things come to be valued as heritage and other things do not has long been a central concern of critical heritage studies. This chapter introduces one of the key ways in which heritage value has been generated and sustained in the modern era, namely through the production, circulation and consumption of documents and records. Academics often describe heritage *as a process* whereby certain values and meanings about the past are produced *in the present, for the future*. Documents and records offer an excellent resource for understanding what exactly happens in this process, and what the limitations and possibilities are for thinking about heritage in this way. Such documents and records may include conservation reports, guidebooks, architectural surveys, visitor studies, interpretation plans, or any other official or unofficial written artefact generated in the heritage-making process. Some of these will be very technical; others may be creative or highly personal. Understanding how to analyse, contextualise and interpret such resources is important for many different types of heritage research, even those that do not explicitly focus on archives or other documentary records. The 'Teaching' section outlines some methods for dealing with these resources, while the 'Praxis' section indicates how researchers have critically examined documents and records in their own work. First, however, it is important to understand why documents and records have come to play such a central role in heritage thinking and practice.

In 2011, while working as a researcher for a heritage consultancy, I was given an unenviable task: review and assess an informal library of reports produced over the previous two decades in relation to a medieval manor house and small museum managed by a local council in North London. On a sunny day in June I was shown to a dusty storeroom, where piles of documents, booklets, reports and folders were stacked on filing cabinets filled with yet more paperwork. I emerged at the end of the day with a spreadsheet going back several years, detailing the varied evaluations and recommendations written for and about the site. I doubt this was the kind of 'archive' Pierre Nora had in mind when he outlined his well-known theory of *lieux de mémoire* ('places of memory'), but here was the detritus of the modern heritage industry: an accumulation of plans and studies documenting the administrative and technical processes involved in managing and – crucially – developing the site.

Although celebrated as a place of great historical significance for decades if not centuries, it could be argued that the heritage *value* of the manor house in question was to some extent produced and sustained through these records. This is not to say the varied buildings making up the site would have been left to fall into ruin without such mundane texts, but their status as heritage assets – with all the undertones of economic worth this term implies – did rely to a certain degree on the constant (re)production of reports, plans, policies and statements generated through many hours of official and unofficial labour (especially true in the context of a local government bureaucracy).

Conservation surveys, funding applications, policy briefings, expert evaluations, statements of significance: the modern heritage industry generates such documents and records at an increasingly frantic pace. In this, however, heritage practice merely reflects a much broader historical trend, namely the discursive and archival formation of modernity writ-large (Foucault 1969). As Françoise Choay outlines in *The Invention of the Historic Monument*, between the second half of the sixteenth century and the second quarter of the nineteenth century, a vast 'iconographic apparatus' emerged to help transform ruins and old buildings into 'antiquities' and 'monuments', with 'a corpus of buildings, conserved by the power of image and text alone … reassembled in a museum of paper' (1992, 41). This form of knowledge production prioritised recorded observations over oral tradition, a development comparable to the empiricism of the natural sciences, which aspired to a 'controllable, and thus reliable, description of its objects' (1992, 51). Documents and records are not *essential* for the production of heritage value, but they are emblematic of a particular form of heritage making, one in which lists, catalogues, surveys and registers play a central role.

Such processes ostensibly seek to document reality, but we must recognise that claims about documentary value and the need to record certain things also *shape* truth and reality. In this sense documents and records constitute heritage, rather than simply reflecting predetermined attitudes and beliefs. In Foucauldian terms, we would say that heritage documents reflect 'the local sociohistorical material conditions that enable and constrain disciplinary knowledge practices such as speaking, writing, thinking, calculating, measuring, filtering, and concentrating. Discursive practices produce, rather than merely describe, the "subjects" and "objects" of knowledge practices' (Barad 2003, 819). Documents and records then offer an important resource for critically examining such discursive practices as they operate in and on the world.

The epistemological roots of this method (really a suite of interconnected methods and analytical techniques, as I explain below) can be located both in structuralist concerns with 'hidden' systems of meaning and post-structuralist enquiries into the effects and limitations of such meaning-making processes. Researchers in cultural studies (Hall 1997), cultural analysis (Bal 1985, 1994), memory studies (Keightley and Pickering 2013), history (Edwards 2022), visual anthropology (Pink 2006; Banks and Zeitlyn 2015) and media studies (Stokes 2013) have drawn variously on textual analysis, visual analysis, semiotics and discourse analysis to (critically) investigate the production, circulation and consumption of diverse materials, from advertisements to family photo albums. Such work must also contend with the fact that most if not all cultural products combine different media, which means paying close attention to language use, imagery, materiality, design and the complex relationships between these elements. Furthermore, any individual 'product' must be understood within its broader socio-cultural context. As Edward Said explained in one of the foundational works deploying this method:

> *The real issue is whether indeed there can be a true representation of anything, or whether any and all representations, because they* are *representations, are embedded first in the language and then in the culture, institutions, and political ambience of the representer. (1978, 272, emphasis in original)*

Documents and records in this reading emerge as complex, multivalent research objects. They are open to a broad range of methods and analytical techniques, touching on questions of visuality, discourse, materiality, semiotics, narrative and many other issues besides. For students and researchers in critical heritage studies, information that falls under this category (e.g. reports, statements, guidebooks) will often form a starting point for wider investigations into the social and political dimensions of heritage, but there are benefits to dwelling on such material rather than taking it at face value. The key point here will be to understand the kind of work that documents and records perform in different heritage processes, how they actively shape rather than simply reflect certain values and meanings, and the role they play within broader heritage practices.

PRAXIS

The types of documents and reports I am interested in here – and that might form the basis for a heritage research project – are distinct from, though often connected to, archival records. As Sven Spieker explains in his book *The Big Archive*, it is important to differentiate between paperwork that circulates within administrative systems and still serves some organisational purpose and the archive proper, which in its original formation 'confined itself to the storage of those records that had been taken out of circulation because they were no longer needed for the dispatch of ongoing business' (2008, 21). Doing research about heritage may involve going into archives to reconstruct historical processes and narratives, but when said processes are part of 'ongoing business' the resources in question often have a very different character: disorganised, ad-hoc, informal and frequently quite banal.[1] Such material precedes and exceeds the archive, forming a documentary infrastructure that offers partial evidence of heritage making in action.

The questions that might be asked of specific documents and records in any heritage research project will depend on the overarching aims and objectives of the study. For example, an interest in the visualisation and marketing of a particular site may lead to a very different set of questions from a study focused on the role of local communities in managing or protecting the same location (although there are likely to be overlaps between such research agendas). Here it is worth remembering that a research methodology will typically be built around three core elements: a distinct research question (or set of questions); a strategy for how evidence will be gathered/generated and analysed to address this question; and a theoretical framework that places the study in context and provides a point of departure for the analysis and conclusions. The second element is where precise research methods come into play, which should always respond to the specific questions being asked. In the case of work focused on documents and records, we might ask: Who produced the documents, and to what ends? What claims do they make about heritage, and what specific tools do they use to build such claims ('tools' here may include photographs, visualisations, charts, diagrams and of course text)? How have the records circulated through different channels, and what impact have they had on the world? Answering such questions will often require a diverse range of methods, where a close attention to distinct documents and records forms part of a broader research strategy encompassing other types of evidence and modes of analysis.

Within my own research on photography and heritage I have often found that the best approach is to draw on multisited methods that try and capture the different ways meaning flows and accrues around diverse documentary processes and resources (see Sterling 2014, 2016, 2020). A useful structure for such research can be found in Gillian Rose's work on visual methodologies, which outlines three 'sites' at which the meanings of an image are made: 'the site(s) of the production of an image, the site of the image itself, and the site(s) where it is seen by various audiences' (2007, 13). While this approach is specifically addressed at visual material (photographs, films, paintings, sketches, maps etc.) the framework is clearly applicable to a wider range of documentary sources, including the kinds of practical literature described in the previous section. This is because any document goes through a similar process, from production through to circulation and interpretation. Moreover, as Rose suggests (2007, 13), each of these sites opens onto a further set of attributes that may be investigated to develop a critical understanding of the material in question, which may be summarised as *technological*, *compositional* and *social* (Rose calls these 'modalities'). Here it should be noted that rather than corresponding to a particular phase or moment of meaning-making, these modalities form an important aspect of analysis at each site. For instance, the production of photographic images in the nineteenth century and the (re)use of those same images in the twenty-first century can both be understood in relation to specific technological apparatuses (chemical, digital or otherwise), deployed within particular socio-cultural contexts (e.g. colonialism, tourism, decolonial exhibition practices; see Sterling 2021 for further details). The same may be said of any image and – by extension – any documentary material.

Let me give an example. Nominating a site for inclusion on the UNESCO World Heritage List requires the production of a detailed dossier. This will include a wide range of historical and contextual information, supported by technical drawings, photographs, maps, visualisations and diagrams. Such documents effectively distil the knowledge, opinions and interpretations of various actors gathered over a long time span (often several years) to satisfy criteria outlined by UNESCO and the three advisory bodies of the World Heritage Convention (ICCROM, ICOMOS and IUCN). Analysing the dossier itself – corresponding to the site of the image in Rose's framework – may involve close reading, visual analysis, discourse analysis or some combination of these methods. It may also mean considering the dossier as a material object, paying attention to 'shape and volume, weight and texture' (Rose 2007, 219).[2] This approach will only allow you to gather a certain depth of evidence, however. The site of production, on the other hand, opens out onto a much broader set of issues and methods, especially interviews or ethnographic research with the people involved in commissioning and writing the report, and background research into the social, political and economic conditions under which the dossier was produced. Finally, the fact such documents are written with a very particular audience in mind underlines the importance of the site of reception and interpretation. How is the dossier ultimately read? Through what networks does it circulate and how is it put to work in different contexts? Again, these questions may be addressed through a range of methods, from quantitative surveys to participant observation (Meskell 2013, 2018; see Melhuish, Degen and Rose 2016 and Rose and Degen 2022 for an example of how Rose herself applies such methods).

Clearly this multisited approach will not be suited to all documentary material. The key point, however, is to recognise that no matter how unassuming, the meaning and value afforded to all documents and records will be contingent upon similar processes and structuring mechanisms. Choosing which analytical site to focus on, and which modalities to prioritise, represents an important step in developing a broader research methodology around such evidence.

TEACHING

How might such questions and concerns be addressed in the classroom? Consider the stack of material described at the start of this chapter. Individually, the varied documents I encountered in the storeroom could be read in quite a straightforward manner, as sources of evidence about the kinds of heritage activities undertaken at the site in question. This would allow for a detailed historical narrative to be compiled, one that would no doubt satisfy research focused on the development and (potential) implementation of certain approaches at the site (in terms of conservation, interpretation and visitor management, for example). Critical heritage studies, however, typically seeks to answer a wider set of questions related to the political, social and ethical dimensions of such work. To what extent can individual documents and records speak to these issues? How might such evidence – as part of a broader research methodology – address the multifaceted dynamics at play in any heritage process?

As a distinct category of evidence, documents and records point in multiple methodological directions at once. This, however, will be true of most sources, which may be approached through a variety of methods depending on the research question(s) to be addressed. Teaching students how to engage with such material may nevertheless benefit from a few key starting points. For example, looking at different specimens of the same type of document (e.g. conservation plans, World Heritage nominations) may help to demonstrate the range of choices that go into the production of even the most banal report. Here, students might focus on issues such as layout, language use, images, authorship and typographic design. Bringing concrete real-world examples of management plans, statements of significance, surveys and other heritage-related documents into the classroom also helps to demonstrate the kinds of work that students themselves may well be asked to undertake in the future. Understanding how such resources are planned, designed and produced can ground abstract discussions of heritage value creation and meaning-making. They are also perfect arenas in which to apply complementary methods related to discourse and visual analysis (see Waterton 2009). While heritage processes cannot be reduced to issues of representation and discourse, recognising how certain claims are made and subsequently codified within official texts – especially policy documents – is often revealing. At the same time, working backwards and forwards from specific documents to consider issues of production, circulation and interpretation is vital to address the work that such material performs in the world. Indeed, heritage practices are often determined by the technocratic demand to produce highly specific documentation for particular audiences, from funding bodies to local community groups. Identifying how and why such documents emerge, and the role they play in establishing and supporting specific arguments about heritage, will represent an important point of departure for many research projects.

It is often difficult to determine with any great certainty the direct impact that certain texts – be they official or unofficial – have on broader material and social worlds. There is not always a clear line between what is written down or illustrated and the bearing such records have on reality. Like most social and cultural phenomena, heritage processes typically unfold through complex and nebulous feedback loops rather than straightforward mandates and effects. Nevertheless, looking at and analysing documents that relate to such processes can help to trace the diverse ways in which heritage is created, negotiated and contested across different social and cultural contexts. Indeed, we might think of such resources as nodal sites where specific ways of thinking about and mobilising heritage are made manifest and put into practice. Such processes do not begin and end with the document. Instead, it is better to see the document as a moment of crystallisation where certain ideas and agendas are placed in a particular configuration, which may be unsettled again by the reader or the next iteration of the same document. By critically analysing such resources students can extract valuable information about how heritage meanings are generated and evolve in relation to distinct social, cultural, political and economic conditions. Here I see an affinity with Ann Stoler's commitment to reading 'along the grain' of colonial archives (2009). This approach, which requires 'a less assured and perhaps more humble stance' to archives (2009, 50), attends to the conventions, expectations and principles through which colonial power impressed itself on diverse social worlds (and indeed continues to do so). As Stoler writes,

> *I treat archives not as repositories of state power but as unquiet movements in a field of force, as restless realignments and readjustments of people and the beliefs to which they were tethered, as spaces in which the senses and the affective course through the seeming abstractions of political rationalities. (Stoler 2009, 33)*

This approach requires careful, patient and meticulous work, something that will also apply to any critical analysis of material still circulating as part of ongoing heritage processes. The difference with this latter category of material, however, is that researchers and students often have the benefit of following their emergence and effects in situ, as they move through the world and become entangled with various social phenomena. The rationalities and realignments of heritage praxis may be usefully unpacked by attending to such sites of evidence.

NOTES

1. Many archives are also like this, of course, but their fundamental 'business' pertains to the production of historical knowledge rather than the continued functioning of a particular project or administrative unit.
2. On this note it is telling that the official guidelines for preparing a World Heritage nomination include the following advice: 'Some nominations are provided in an elaborate and special box. While packaging the information in a box can be practically convenient, it is the quality of the information which is important, not the quality of the packaging' (UNESCO 2011, 97).

REFERENCES AND RESOURCES

Bal, Mieke. 1985. *Narratology: Introduction to the theory of narrative*. Toronto: University of Toronto Press.

Bal, Mieke. 1994. *On Meaning-Making: Essays in semiotics*. Sonoma, CA: Polebridge Press.

Banks, Marcus and David Zeitlyn. 2015. *Visual Methods in Social Research*. 2nd ed. London: Sage.

Barad, Karen. 2003. 'Posthumanist performativity: Toward an understanding of how matter comes to matter'. *Signs: Journal of Women in Culture and Society* 28(3): 801–31.

Choay, Françoise. 1992 [2001]. *The Invention of the Historic Monument*. L. M. O'Connell (trans.). Cambridge: Cambridge University Press.

Degen, Monia Montserrat and Gillian Rose. 2022. *The New Urban Aesthetic: Digital experiences of urban change*. London: Bloomsbury.

Edwards, Elizabeth. 2022. *Photographs and the Practice of History*. London: Bloomsbury.

Foucault, Michel. 1969 [2011]. *The Archaeology of Knowledge*. A. M. Sheridan Smith (trans.). London: Routledge.

Hall, Stuart (ed.) 1997. *Representation: Cultural representations and signifying practices*. London: Sage.

Keightley, Emily and Michael Pickering (eds) 2013. *Research Methods for Memory Studies*. Edinburgh: Edinburgh University Press.

Melhuish, Clare, Monica Degen and Gillian Rose. 2016. '"The real modernity that is here": Understanding the role of digital visualisations in the production of a new urban imaginary at Msheireb Downtown, Doha'. *City and Society* 28(2): 222–45.

Meskell, Lynn. 2013. 'UNESCO's World Heritage Convention at 40: Challenging the economic and political order of international heritage conservation'. *Current Anthropology* 54(4): 483–94.

Meskell, Lynn. 2018. *A Future in Ruins: UNESCO, World Heritage, and the dream of peace*. Oxford: Oxford University Press.

Nora, Pierre. 1989. 'Between memory and history: *Les lieux de mémoire*'. *Representations* 26 (Spring): 7–24.

Pink, Sarah. 2006. *The Future of Visual Anthropology: Engaging the senses*. Oxford: Routledge.

Rose, Gillian. 2007. *Visual Methodologies: An introduction to the interpretation of visual materials*. 2nd ed. London: Sage.

Said, Edward. 1978 [2003]. *Orientalism*. London: Penguin.

Spieker, Sven. 2008 [2017]. *The Big Archive: Art from bureaucracy*. London: The MIT Press.

Sterling, Colin. 2014. 'Photography, preservation and ethics at Angkor'. *Future Anterior* 11(1): 70–83.

Sterling, Colin. 2016. 'Mundane myths: Heritage and the politics of the photographic cliché'. *Public Archaeology* 15(2–3): 87–112.

Sterling, Colin. 2020. *Heritage, Photography, and the Affective Past*. London: Routledge.

Sterling, Colin. 2021. 'Emergent images: Matters of affect in heritage photography'. In *Heritage Ecologies*, edited by Þóra Pétursdóttir and Torgeir Rinke Bangstad, 107–28. London: Routledge.

Stokes, Jane. 2013. 'Researching texts: Approaches to analysing media and cultural content'. In *How to Do Media and Cultural Studies*, edited by Jane Stokes, 118–69. London: Sage.

Stoler, Ann Laura. 2009. *Along the Archival Grain: Epistemic anxieties and colonial common sense*. Princeton, NJ: Princeton University Press.

UNESCO. 2011. *Preparing World Heritage Nominations*. 2nd ed. Paris: UNESCO.

Waterton, Emma. 2009. 'Sights of sites: Picturing heritage, power and exclusion'. *Journal of Heritage Tourism* 4(1): 37–56.

Waterton, Emma and Steve Watson. 2014. *The Semiotics of Heritage Tourism*. Bristol: Channel View Publications.

4 On refusal (to record)

Uzma Z. Rizvi

Why does research require discovery and collection?

Is there some way for us to imagine a different way of being in the world?

Refusal is both an analytic and a methodological intervention: it is, in its essence, a different way of being in the world. In this short piece, I present refusal as an interruption to the status quo – a methodological praxis that disrupts and stops engagement with systems of oppression. In the simplest and most profound sense, this method is about saying no; it is to object. Importantly, it is also about respecting consent if the people you are working with refuse your interlocution. As a way to model an ethical praxis, I will only present methodologies that I have engaged in myself, so that the reader has a clear sense that such refusal is, indeed, something possible to do. And, importantly, that refusal can be generative rather than extractive. This latter point is significant as we are taught that the only way research happens or is considered worthy is if it fulfils our expectations of a complete study. What this contribution is asking is to consider the many different ways of recognising research value while also centring a consent-based, non-harmful method that recognises and respects the humanity of the communities we work with/in.

I began work in the United Arab Emirates (UAE) in 2012, with a plan to do archaeological survey work and then excavations. By 2013, I began my work with a detailed collection study of Harappan (and non-Harappan) materials in the various museum collections and whatever I could access in terms of excavation storage. As I met with the various government officials to talk through test trenches as a part of my survey, it became clear that permits for excavations were provided with certain attendant details. One of those details was labour. With the permit I would receive a car, an apartment, an appropriate amount of labour and equipment. I mentioned that I could take care of everything else, I just needed the permit, and that seemed to be a bureaucratic and technical issue. I mentioned that I would be fine with everything else, but I did not want to engage in 'employing' Gulf labour. By the end of the year, I sat down with one of the archaeologists who was in charge of the first round of approvals for the permit in Sharjah, and I learnt that at that time there would be no way for me to do archaeological work without using the labour provided by the state.

In 2017, I had an interesting conversation with a senior European archaeologist at the site of Harappa in Pakistan. We were both there for a conference, and this archaeologist works in the UAE as well, and they asked me, as so many others have, when I would start my excavations in Sharjah and why I had not started yet. I explained how I was still trying to figure out a way to use a different kind of labour for excavations. To which they first responded with an understanding nod and a yes, the workers are not so great but you can train them, especially since *you* have the language skills as *you* come from the same place they do (referring to our shared South Asian descent – and yes, this was a problematic comment, but this is not about me). I responded, correcting them because it was not at all an issue of excavation skills, but rather that the people who are the excavation labour force are from the same labour pool as that for construction, who are all part of a neocolonial and imperial transnational labour flow of disenfranchised bodies without many rights. As bodies caught in a system with subcontractors who extract money from them at every step, they are now bound in precarious situations in which they owe more money than they will ever be able to pay off and are now bound to a lifetime of servitude for the subcontractor. We ended that conversation with me saying that I refused to excavate using the UAE-provided labour. As a methodological consideration, if a policy or a way of working is inequitable to others who are in a disenfranchised condition, I recommend we not accept those conditions of work just to further our research. I continued to show up in the UAE and I continued *not* to dig. Just in the same way one might, knowingly or unknowingly, reiterate a system of colonial inequity by not taking a decolonial approach to their work, by exercising a right of refusal I keep reminding myself of resistance to an imperial logic that underlies much archaeological work done around the world.

The years between 2013 and 2018 I showed up every year and did archaeology – but what that archaeology looked like was a refusal of excavation that would replicate inequitable systems and reinstate neocolonial and imperial forms of oppression; it also looked like me not talking or writing about Gulf labour and the community-based activism that was transforming society because my interlocutors explicitly refused to be subjects of research. And I respected their refusal. These politics of refusal came to the surface through collaborative discursive and critical pedagogical experiences in Dubai and Sharjah – two of the Emirates in the UAE where I had been living, working, thinking, eating, drinking, writing and coproducing research with collaborators for nearly a decade.

What set this analytic of refusal in motion was the recognition that I was working within the Global South in order to extract information for the Global North academy. If archaeology was not extractive enough, the violence of this act was made apparent when my collaborators explicitly said they were not interested in being subjects for the American academy – nor were they interested in engagement if it was in the service of *my* research. My stakes within my own work and understanding of the world shifted with these conversations and I understood Edward Said's wisdom with regard to what it might mean to write about a place and what it might mean to write in and for a place.

Alongside clarity around my standpoint, these experiences also instructed me on how to navigate and make relevant archaeology and heritage in trans-disciplinary spaces. This, in turn, provided the possibility of imagining different futures for our disciplines. It made me realise that knowledge about the past, about heritage, about antiquity was unbounded, infinite and not there for us, as practitioners, to control. But rather, the rigorous and interesting research that made us think about the world differently emerged through relationships and consent.

> *The goal of refusal is not for objects to become subjects in the academy, but contrarily, to* ***object to*** *the very processes of objectification/subjection, the making of possessors and possessions, the alchemy of becoming-claims. (Tuck and Yang 2014, 814, emphasis in original)*

REFERENCES AND RESOURCES

Ortner, Sherry B. 1995. 'Resistance and the problem of ethnographic refusal'. *Comparative Studies in Society and History* 37(1): 173–93.

Simpson, Audra. 2016. 'Consent's revenge'. *Cultural Anthropology* 31(3): 326–33.

Tuck, Eve and K. Wayne Yang. 2014. 'Unbecoming claims: Pedagogies of refusal in qualitative research'. *Qualitative Inquiry* 20(6): 811–18.

5 Archives and historiography

Laura McAtackney

DESCRIPTION AND HISTORIOGRAPHY

Some of the most influential texts we associate with the formation of heritage studies as a coherent, interdisciplinary subject – which many date from the mid-1980s (Gentry and Smith 2019) – were driven by issues of how we know, think about, write about and present the relationship between the past *as it is* entangled with the present. Seminal volumes such as David Lowenthal's *The Past is a Foreign Country* (1985) and Patrick Wright's *On Living in an Old Country* (1985) were significant in providing theoretical framings and critical analyses of processes that were especially relevant because they were playing out in contemporary society. By observing the expanded role of the so-called heritage industry in dealing with wholescale changes in post/industrial 'Western' societies, early heritage scholars provided thoughtful critiques of 'heritage' being used as a problematic, nostalgic response to mask wider social changes. Lowenthal (2015, updated), who was both a geographer and historian, placed a strong emphasis on the unknowability of the past and how it was always being reconfigured for present needs. This stance stood in contrast to the heritage industry in practice, which he argued used nostalgia for disappearing traditional industries to claim accessibility to that past through preservation and interpretation. His early and influential musings exploring the role of key sources and methods in heritage – documents, memory, material culture, place – and critically assessing their contributions to connecting the past with the present remain hugely important (Gentry and Smith 2019). But in exploring these early writings, it is clear that Lowenthal often conflated 'history' with the past rather than distinguishing it from the discipline concerned with written records and archives as sources.

The role of persistent and 'authentic' material remains have been key to connecting the past with the contemporary for both the heritage industry and heritage studies but there is a need to question exactly what this means. Siân Jones has explored authenticity (2010) through traditional definitions, which centre on material integrity, to more constructivist ideas that highlight the role of social and intangible meaning in determining authenticity. This is a useful distinction to consider when exploring the role of archives and historiography in heritage studies, especially in questioning the naturalisation of archives as unchanging remnants when in reality they are continually being reconstructed in the present (Swain 2003; Taylor 2018; Kryder-Reid 2018). These issues become most prominent when working with 'difficult' or 'dark' heritage in which there are few agreed narratives about what constituted the past and contestation about how they continue to shape our understandings in the present. Whereas the potential role of archives in providing insights into the past – be they documentary or oral; paper-based or digital – have been explored in historical studies and anthropology, they have not been prominent in heritage studies. This is despite the need to consider epistemological issues of knowledge creation and formation as both a top-down and bottom-up phenomenon in using various types of archives to work with heritage issues. For heritage researchers working with difficult heritage, in particular, there has been a tendency to bypass critical engagement with official, paper-based archives as a source and to instead focus on bottom-up 'community archives' (see Flinn, Stevens and Shepherd 2009) to better represent historically marginalised experiences. For example, Indigenous communities in settler colonial societies such as Canada have reacted to government reports acknowledging settler colonial harm by collecting their own oral histories and increasingly pressurising for acceptance of what Taylor calls 'the status and legitimacy of Indigenous epistemologies and ways of learning about the past and, more broadly, the status of historical memory and memory studies' (2018, 218). But even within societies that do not have governmental acknowledgement of historical, systemic marginalisation there can be widespread distrust of official archives, and especially governmental records, in directing our understandings of the past. This is because the traditional role of such repositories has been to document and legitimate the state, which results in the sidelining and marginalisation of experiences that are not mainstream. In practice, the communities who are essentially 'hidden from history' (Hodgkin and Radstone 2005, 11) often become the focus of critical heritage research.

The term 'archival' often presumes an official – usually state or governmental – role that involves a recognised institution that collects, classifies and catalogues papers before making them accessible to the public. Such official archives are often highly structured places whose primary role is to maintain selected records – and construct official narratives – of the state, although this presumption does not mean that those archives cannot be used to reveal other realities (see Anderson 2011; McAtackney 2014). In considering the role of archival approaches to heritage studies it is especially important to reflect on the ambiguity of the term heritage and the distinctions that can be made between *official* and *unofficial* heritage (including Harrison 2013) – or authorised and unauthorised (Smith 2006) – in ways that also extend to archives. Archives can also be grassroots, unofficial and counter-hegemonic enterprises, created in response to blind spots and deficits of the state, or simply to allow communities or collectives to bring together their own cultural memory (Flinn, Stevens and Shepherd 2009; Hamber and Kelly 2016). Stoler (2002), Flewellen (2019) and others have shown that colonial archives, in particular, benefit from both broad conceptualisation and detailed reflection in order to move beyond official narratives.

Other forms of archives that are increasingly popular, and allow for more critical engagement in heritage studies, are oral archives and digital archives. Oral archives grew in prominence from the mid-twentieth century for different reasons globally. In Europe, they can be traced to a reaction against the traumas of World War II and the Cold War and in post/colonial contexts the emphasis on grassroots movements, everyday experience and marginalised experience was viewed as a necessary corrective to

Eurocentric models (Craggs 2018). While oral archives have been important means of diversifying our knowledge and access to the past, critics had long questioned the accuracy of memory as a factual, historical source. Oral historians such as Portelli (1981) and Frisch (1990) have instead placed the role of subjectivity and changeability as a primary asset and this is a key attribute when being used for heritage research. Digital archives are increasingly important due to the promise of accessibility, regardless of the format of the archive. All forms of archive have a role to play in heritage studies but it is important to remember that archives close to power should reflect on their role in upholding structural inequalities in the past through to the present day. Jarrett M. Drake (2016) and others have critiqued the desire of official archives to address systemic racism in response to the Black Lives Matter movement. He argues that unless official archives recognise their complicity in upholding patriarchy and white supremacy, and work through the long process of building trust with communities and grassroots organisations, they should simply desist.

In many ways, archival modes of accessing the past have been sidelined from heritage studies, particularly within what has become known as critical heritage studies (CHS). Gentry and Smith's (2019) historiography of heritage studies has questioned how much CHS has deviated from the early preoccupations of the field with tangibles and memory (see Introduction and Chapter 7). Building on Gentry and Smith's (2019, 1152) argument that CHS builds on influences from archaeology, architecture and geography (2019, 1152), it seems clear that archival engagements with the past have not been explicitly critical to either study. Why is this? I argue it is due to both forms of heritage studies implicitly positioning themselves away from history as the key disciplinary lens onto the past to allow for a focus on the political context of heritage as a study of the present through the past. In contrast to historical and archival approaches, the interdisciplinarity of heritage studies was conceived as a broader and more holistic way to know the past than traditional archival and documentary approaches but this means that archives have not been as critically assessed as they deserved to be.

PRAXIS

Natalie Zemon Davis (2010) has argued that the 'past always recedes' from those wholly reliant on documents to understand history and clearly there are notable limitations in using archives to research and write about all but the most elite and mainstream heritage. But this does not mean that archival approaches to heritage need to follow the traditional 'sanctity of the archive' or be limited to collections of papers. Rather, archival approaches to heritage can critically engage with documents as sources that require reflection and interrogation and they can envision archives in non-paper form, especially oral and digital.

To exemplify the many layers and complexities of working with archives from a heritage perspective, I focus on the roles, potential and limitations of various forms of archives associated with the recent conflict in Northern Ireland, colloquially known as 'the Troubles' (c.1968 to c.1998). As one might expect in such a longstanding, recent and enduringly contentious period of conflict, there is a wide range of heritage research related to the Northern Irish conflict. Topics covered range from critically assessing the connection between community and heritage (Crooke 2007), the role of the official heritage of museums (Crooke 2023) and the unofficial heritage of paramilitary museums (Markham 2018) through to the potential of peace-oriented place-making (McAtackney 2013) and explorations of the proliferation of grassroots memorials on the streets where conflict happened (Viggiani 2014). Many heritage-related texts focus on heritage institutions, especially museums, and there has been critical engagement with the role and impacts of archives in knowing and constructing the past, especially bottom-up oral archives created to reflect the experiences of marginalised or overlooked groups (Moloney 2013; Roulston 2017). While there are many advocates for the potential of oral archives to give voice to 'history from below', especially those most often marginalised from historical discourse on conflict (i.e. women, children [Bryson 2021]), there has been criticism of the overemphasis on oral archives due to issues with ethics, practices and unforeseen outcomes for a number of projects. The most high-profile examples include the so-called

Boston College tape controversy, in which presumed sensitive materials were recorded by the coordinators of the oral archive (an ex-combatant and a journalist) and subsequently became the subject of security agency subpoena (Breen-Smyth 2020), and an ESRC-project collapsing due to the inclusion within the ethics paperwork of an intention to share intelligence with British security agencies (without the consent of the researcher employed or the focus group under study: dissident republicans [Hayes and McIntyre 2014]). These types of controversies have prompted critical assessments of oral history archives by historians and legal scholars but they do not tend to occupy heritage researchers, who have rather focused on heritage institutions, landscapes and/or material culture in their studies (see Crooke and Maguire 2018).

The role of official, paper-based archives is largely unarticulated in heritage studies approaches to the conflict in Northern Ireland, with critical engagement with archives largely left to historians (who still tend to dominate public understandings of how the past is remembered in Ireland [Bryan 2022]) or lawyers. This oversight is puzzling for a number of reasons. Public archives are official heritage institutions that hold immense power in determining what past is available, known and constructed by not only historians but any other disciplines interested in the recent past. In the case of Northern Ireland, official archives have a particularly complicated role due to the official lack of 'dealing with the past' (McGrattan 2013) included in the transition to peace. This means there is no consensus about the origins of the conflict, cause and effect throughout the 30 years it endured, and what its legacies are, and so the role of official, governmental archives requires careful consideration. While there are historians who continue to claim the role as neutral arbiter (McBride 2017), this position is contested in Northern Ireland (Burke 2019). Far from receding with passing time, debate about the conflict has been enlivened due to what Ian McBride has called memory becoming 'a war by other means' (McBride 2018). This situation has only heightened in the post-Brexit referendum context with the constitutional status of the North becoming unsettled due to the focus on the border between Northern Ireland and Ireland and with the recent imposition of the deeply unpopular Northern

Ireland Troubles (Legacy and Reconciliation) Bill (2023) by the Westminster government. For the latter, despite opposition from civic society in Northern Ireland, the so-called Legacy Bill has been pushed through parliament in London. Among its many aims are to complete an official history of the conflict based on British government archives while closing down investigations into unresolved cases, many of which involved British state agents (NIHRC 2022).

Alongside this fluctuating and volatile context there are other factors that also complicate completing archival research on the conflict, including the dispersed nature of the archives. Official archives relating to Northern Ireland can be found in three main state repositories: the Public Record Office of Northern Ireland (PRONI, Belfast), The National Archives (TNA, Kew) and the National Archives of Ireland (NAI, Dublin). This tripartite arrangement is not equal or intentional, with the majority of official records relating to the operation of government in Northern Ireland divided – and often replicated – between Belfast and London, reflecting the realities of direct rule from Westminster between 1972 and 1998. This situation resulted in government offices existing in Belfast or London, as well as coexisting between both locations, and creating their own distinct but entangled archives. The archive in Dublin exists because the Republic of Ireland retained a constitutional claim over Northern Ireland through articles 2 and 3 of its 1937 constitution, which became an official role in governance with the Anglo-Irish Agreement (1985), and only ended as a consequence of the Good Friday Agreement (1998). Added complications arise from different archival practices across the three sites in terms of how files have been assessed for retention or destruction, accessed and catalogued, timescales for opening to the public and interpretations as to enduring sensitivity.

The messy reality of completing archival work on the Northern Irish conflict can be used to reflect on the role of archives in critical heritage research more generally, including a need to critically engage in a more systemic way with their knowledge claims rather than that nebulous but oft-repeated claim of reading 'against their [archival] grain' (Stoler 2002: 99). When I started conducting research on Long Kesh/Maze prison for a PhD, 2004–2008, I had a background as an archaeologist, heritage professional and I had worked as an archivist in PRONI. As a researcher I had time to critically reflect on how that particular archive worked and this included questioning practices and processes that should have provoked more reflection while I was an employee. One key issue in hindsight was the lack of transparency and oversight regarding what files departments produced versus what we were asked to review. One of my roles at PRONI was to review departmental closed files as they were presented to us. We would often arrive at sites with no clear prior understanding of what files existed or what decisions were made about when and how files were closed. Some departments had large archives of their own and we could access a substantial number and range of files that covered significantly different subject areas (e.g. health); other departments had a number of mini-archives that were site specific (planning within the Department of Environment); some government departments requested our services relatively frequently (Education), while others were clearly hostile to our involvement and provided very limited access to the department and their files (Northern Ireland Office). When files were eventually forwarded to PRONI for retention, some did not appear (the Court Service were expected to transfer any files on conflict-related deaths, but when systematic searches for particular groups of deaths were completed there were often significant numbers of missing files) and others were significantly 'weeded' between files closure and accessioning at the state archive. It was clear that without overarching systems and structures in place the archive had a lack of oversight in terms of what it held and how its collections reflected the files that original existed.

I reflected on how one could make sense of these files from a heritage, or even history, point of view and part of that process was dealing with the different types of issues in making sense of the past in our moving moment of the present. When I went to TNA to examine their files I found I could access files related to the 1981 Hunger Strikes, one of the most controversial series of events associated with the conflict, which either did not exist, were in different filing configurations or were not yet opened at PRONI. It is clear that in recent years, questions about past actions, especially those related to state actors, whose conduct was not thoroughly investigated at the time, continue to impact on archival practice. For example, it was reported in 2019 that TNA at Kew had greatly extended the closure period for files relating to deaths and injuries from plastic bullets shot by police and soldiers during the conflict. This included files related to the death of Julie Livingstone, who was 14 when she was killed in 1981 by a plastic bullet, and whose file closure was extended in 2019 for a further 45 years for ambiguous reasons related to 'health and safety' and 'personal information where the application is a 3rd party' (Irish News 2019). These discrepancies reflected the fact that the archives had different regimes of knowledge, timescales for opening files and ideas about the sensitivities versus public interest in the subject that were being constantly negotiated in the present. Across the three archives I found that locating relevant files was a haphazard task; files relating to Long Kesh/Maze could appear in any number of departments, and there was often relevant material in files with names that did not appear to be relevant to the prison (and vice versa, nothing relevant in files that related to prisons). The contents of files included expected contents that were clearly related to the file name, some that were somewhat connected to the broad theme but included a wide range of inclusions, and others that were completely dissonant collections of papers. It became increasingly clear that for a heritage of this prison to include the official archives, they needed to be critically and transparently assessed. Following Ann Laura Stoler they had to be contextualised from a postcolonial positionality. The files that were created by regimes that did not fully understand their subject, and 'a move from archive-as-source to archive-as-subject' (2002, 93) was required. I began to explore documents within official archives with the express aim of revealing the mechanisms and assumptions of governance that allowed interpretation and understanding of 'archives not as sites of knowledge retrieval but of knowledge production, as monuments of states as well as sites of state ethnography' (2002, 90). I would extend such advice to any critical heritage scholar utilising official archives, especially when working with more marginalised groups and experiences.

TEACHING

Working with official documentary archives can be bewildering for heritage students, especially if their educational background has prioritised documentary 'history' as the main and overarching means of accessing the past. If documentary archives are one source in a mixed methodology it is important that students are made conscious of how they relate to other sources; for example, materials, places and oral testimonies can all reveal different aspects of any given study. It is extremely easy for archival material to be overly prioritised as the factual hook from which other sources merely become the 'handmaiden to history' (Hume 1964). From a critical heritage perspective, the heritage student often wishes to embrace a more 'bottom-up' perspective in the spirit of challenging or de-centring what Laurajane Smith (2006) has famously termed 'authorized heritage discourse'. In order to not replicate the knowledge and assumptions of official documentary archives there is a need to start with creating a consciousness that (1) biases of power exist in archives in various ways, and (2) documentary archives can, and should, be deconstructed in critical ways.

To start this process, teaching must focus on learning from historians who have explicitly critically assessed the documentary archives and denaturalised its claims to knowledge and power in how we know the past. It can seem a difficult task to navigate archival claims while simultaneously trying to 'unlearn' them, as Ariella Azoulay describes (Azoulay 2019), but it is possible. In my teaching practice I dedicate significant class time at the beginning of courses to deconstructing the archive, and a key starting point is learning from those who have already done so in their research. It is fortunate there has been a rich stream of books in recent years critiquing positivist readings of archives, especially in constructing histories where there are clear power differentials between those creating the archive and those being represented in it. A compelling example is the increasingly nuanced monographs that reveal how we construct and write about colonial and imperial histories from a critical perspective that combines archival with other, often literary, sources (e.g. Gopal 2019; Aiken 2022; Manjapra 2023).

Although pedagogical concerns are not central to most of these books, they do hold a key pedagogical function in being explicit in their critical assessment of the official archive. By questioning the archive through combining various archival and other sources to reveal their contradictions, and by interrogating the anxieties inherent in the archives, they reveal how archival claims of power are open to deconstruction. We must recognise the intended function of the official archive – to record, extract and control people and resources – in order to know, critique and unlearn their biases. Reading such volumes acts as a valuable pedagogical starting point in allowing students to 'see' the power structures, inbuilt biases and prejudices that can otherwise be naturalised. Without an active process of 'unlearning' it is almost impossible for students to use archives in ways that creatively engage with them and question the basis of their knowledge claims and/or their assumptions about those they document as part of their research process.

Once a deep engagement with 'unlearning' processes has been undertaken, the students can be lead through more practical exercises that have pedagogical value in allowing for 'real-world' engagement with archives. In practice, it is often difficult to facilitate access of teaching groups to official archives due to limitations of spaces, which are generally not teaching focused, and issues with slotting such extra-curricular activities into busy teaching timetables. While Breathnach, Mulrennan and Keogh (2021, 610) advocate for using digital resources to allow students to access collections, as part of the MA in Sustainable Heritage Management at Aarhus University we used a 'collection' of photocopies so the students were able to replicate the sensory experience of handling documents in our practical sessions. Working with archives is a small but integral part of the degree and is included in an introductory course on 'Sources and Methods', which includes a diverse group of students, many of whom have no background in history or archival studies. During a three-hour class the students are randomly divided into small working groups of no more than four people who have diverse disciplinary backgrounds and we provide them with the same small collection of papers from an archive. What they are not told is that the collection was the product of a desktop assessment that includes a range of primary and secondary documents relating to a property that was first mentioned in legal documents in the seventeenth century and is associated with the Brown family (of Brown University fame).

At the start of the exercise they are given clear instructions as to the aim of the practical – which is to sort and provisionally catalogue the papers – and they are reminded that they should be critically engaging with the archive rather than overly focusing on fact extracting. It is emphasised that there are no 'right' or 'wrong' answers but they are expected to explain their decision-making processes. To help the groups get the most from the exercise, including questioning the knowledge claims of the collection, they are provided with a number of pointers, with an instruction to list the types of documents included and reflect on why they might be there, to look for contradictory 'factual' information (not all the dates or names contained in the documents are consistent), look for hints as to the social history of the estate (there were various indicators of the presence of Indigenous people, women, children and social changes that were not the aim of the documents but were present), and last to tell us how they would arrange the papers to allow access to an archive user. After a designated amount of time the students were asked to feed back to the rest of the class in their groups and we had discussions about what they learnt. Feedback on the exercise was always positive in terms of the benefits of learning through practice and learning from each other's processes, and they felt they learnt how to read the papers in ways that were not necessarily intended.

Using oral archives, especially from unofficial or grassroots archives, can provide many creative pedagogical possibilities. This is especially the case if the oral material is open access and online. The experiences of the pandemic have prompted much reflection by academics and practitioners working with heritage regarding the possibilities of online and open access oral archives. Kelly and Horan (2021) have detailed the pedagogical benefits they witnessed in creating a collaborative oral archive of the pandemic that allowed students not only to contribute but to shape the oral archive over the course of the first year, which included how they could adapt traditional oral history good practice to the needs of that time. Likewise, Lee and Springer (2020) have revealed how they refocused the critical engagement with oral histories as part of a year-long course on 'Contemporary Civilization' at Colombia University from analysing existing collections to consciously creating their own archives. They emphasised that students explicitly considered their own subjectivities and positionalities and noted how they were transparent as instructors about their limits of knowledge in how to navigate this particular moment of crisis (2020, 230). While many of these innovative uses and approaches to oral archives were specific to the context of pandemic lockdown, they clearly provide useful reflections on how to use and adapt those approaches more generally, especially in allowing students to be archive creators, not just users. Key to their successes was a focus on the archive as a creative, evolving and subjective place that can be critically engaged with as well as shaped by the students working with it.

REFERENCES AND RESOURCES

Resources

This collection of archival resources has been selected to provide opportunities to engage with a range of digital and open access archives in order to consider how they produce knowledge but also contest knowledge within the wider structure of their operation.

CAIN Archive – Conflict and Politics in Northern Ireland: https://cain.ulster.ac.uk

Colonial Caribbean CO Files from TNA: https://www.amdigital.co.uk/collection/colonial-caribbean

Danish West Indies – Sources of History (Rigsarkivet): https://www.virgin-islands-history.org/en/search-the-records/

Digital Schomburg (Schomburg Centre for Research in Black Culture): https://www.nypl.org/about/locations/schomburg/digital-schomburg

Divided Society Northern Ireland 1990–1998 (Linenhall Library Political Collection): https://www.dividedsociety.org
Legacies of British Slavery Database: https://www.ucl.ac.uk/lbs/project/details/
Prison Memory Archive: https://prisonsmemoryarchive.com

References

Aiken, Síobhra. 2022. *Spiritual Wounds: Trauma, testimony and the Irish Civil War*. Dublin: Irish Academic Press.
Anderson, David M. 2011. 'Mau Mau in the High Court and the "lost" British Empire Archives: Colonial conspiracy or bureaucratic bungle?' *The Journal of Imperial and Commonwealth History* 39(5): 699–716.
Azoulay, Ariella Aïsha. 2019. *Potential History: Unlearning imperialism*. London: Verso.
Breathnach, Ciara, Kirsten Mulrennan and Sinéad A. Keogh. 2021. 'Making space: Archival transcribathons and practice-based learning in undergraduate medical history'. *The History Teacher* 54(4): 609–36.
Breen-Smyth, Marie. 2020. 'Interviewing combatants: Lessons from the Boston College Case'. *Contemporary Social Science* 15(2): 258–74.
Bryan, Dominic. 2022. 'Taking the history out of the Decade of Centenaries: Narratives, rituals and symbols in British identities in Northern Ireland'. *Éire/Ireland* 57(1–2): 63–86.
Bryson, Anna. 2021. 'The politics of preservation: Oral history, socio-legal studies, and praxis'. *Journal of Law and Society* 48 (Supp 1): s74–s87.
Burke, Mike. 2019. 'Should we trust Irish historians?' *The Pensive Quill*. Last modified 12 August 2019. Accessed 14 March 2024. https://www.thepensivequill.com/2019/08/should-we-trust-irish-historians.html.
Craggs, Ruth. 2018. 'Subaltern geopolitics and the post-colonial Commonwealth, 1965–1990'. *Political Geography* 65: 46–56.
Crooke, Elizabeth. 2007. *Museums and Community: Ideas, issues and challenges*. London: Routledge.

Crooke, Elizabeth. 2023. 'The challenge of change: Museum practice informed by and informing the peace process'. In *The Routledge Handbook of the Northern Ireland Conflict and Peace*, edited by Laura McAtackney and Máirtín Ó Catháin, 473–87. London: Routledge.

Crooke, Elizabeth and Tom Maguire (eds) 2018. *Heritage After Conflict: Northern Ireland.* London: Routledge.

Drake, Jarrett M. 2016. Expanding #ArchivesForBlackLives to traditional archival repositories. *Medium*. Last modified 27 June 2016. Accessed 14 March 2024. https://medium.com/on-archivy/expanding-archivesforblacklives-to-traditional-archival-repositories-b88641e2daf6#.fr1uexerh

Flewellen, Oyana Omilade. 2019. 'African diasporic choices: Locating the lived experiences of Afro-Crucians in the archival and archaeological record'. *NTIK* 8(2): 54–74.

Flinn, Andrew, Mary Stevens and Elizabeth Shepherd. 2009. 'Whose memories, whose archives? Independent community archives, autonomy and the mainstream'. *Archival Science* 9: 71–86.

Frisch, Michael. 1990. *Essays on the Craft and Meaning of Oral and Public History*. Albany, NY: State University of New York Press.

Gentry, Kynan and Laurajane Smith. 2019. 'Critical heritage studies and the legacies of the late-twentieth century heritage canon'. *International Journal of Heritage Studies* 25(11): 1148–68.

Gopal, Priyamvada. 2019. *Insurgent Empire: Anticolonialism and the making of British dissent*. London: Verso.

Hamber, Brandon and Gráinne Kelly. 2016. 'Practice, power and inertia: Personal narrative, archives and dealing with the past in Northern Ireland'. *Journal of Human Rights Practice* 8(1): 25–44.

Hayes, Mark and Anthony McIntyre. 2014. 'The Liverpool University research project on "dissident" Irish republicanism – working for the British state?' *The Pensive Quill*. Last modified 6 October 2014. Accessed 14 March 2024. https://www.thepensivequill.com/2014/10/the-liverpool-university-research.html.

Hodgkin, Katherine and Susannah Radstone (eds) 2005. *The Politics of Memory: Contested pasts*. Pisatawny, NJ: Transaction.

Hume, Ivor Noel. 1964. 'Archaeology: Handmaiden to history'. *The North Carolina Historical Review* 41(2): 214–25.

Irish News. 2019. 'British government files on plastic bullets closed up to additional 50 years'. 19 April. Accessed 14 March 2024. https://www.irishnews.com/news/northernirelandnews/2019/04/19/news/british-government-files-on-plastic-bullets-closed-up-to-additional-50-years-1601186/.

Jones, Siân. 2010. 'Negotiating authentic objects and authentic selves: Beyond the deconstruction of authenticity'. *Journal of Material Culture* 15(2): 181–203.

Kelly, Jason M. and John Horan. 2021. 'Archive as pedagogy: Oral history and a journal of the plague year'. *Collections* 17(3): 237–46.

Kryder-Reid, Elizabeth. 2018. 'Introduction: Tools for a critical heritage'. *International Journal of Heritage Studies* 24(7): 691–93.

Lee, Ana Paulina and Kimberly Springer. 2020. 'Socially engaged oral history pedagogy amid COVID-19 pandemic'. *The Oral History Review* 47(2): 227–39.

Lowenthal, David. 2015. *The Past is a Foreign Country*. Cambridge: Cambridge University Press.

Manjapra, Kris. 2023. *Black Ghost of Empire: The long death of slavery and the failure of emancipation*. New York: Scribner.

Markham, Katie. 2018. 'Organised innocence in the paramilitary museum'. In *Heritage After Conflict: Northern Ireland*, edited by Elizabeth Crooke and Tom Maguire, 49–65. London: Routledge.

McAtackney, Laura. 2013. 'Sectarianism'. In *The Oxford Handbook of the Archaeology of the Contemporary Past*, edited by Paul Graves-Brown, Rodney Harrison and Angela Piccini, 232–46. Oxford: Oxford University Press.

McAtackney, Laura. 2014. *An Archaeology of the Troubles: The dark heritage of Long Kesh/Maze prison*. Oxford: Oxford University Press.

McBride, Ian. 2017. 'Dealing with the Past: Historians and the Northern Ireland conflict'. Accessed 14 March 2024. https://www.academia.edu/34292402/McBride_Dealing_with_the_Past_2017.pdf.

McBride, Ian. 2018. 'Dealing with the past: History, memory and the Northern Ireland Troubles'. In *History, Memory and Public Life: The past in the present*, edited by Anna Maerker, Simon Sleight and Adam Sutcliffe. London: Routledge.

McGrattan, Cillian. 2013. *Memory, Politics and Identity: Haunted by history*. Basingstoke: Palgrave Macmillan.

Moloney, Michelle. 2013. 'Reaching out from the archive: The role of community oral history archives in conflict transformation in Northern Ireland'. PhD thesis, University of Ulster, Northern Ireland.

Northern Ireland Human Rights Commission (NIHRC). 2022. *Advice on NI Troubles (Legacy and Reconciliation) Bill: September 2022*. Accessed 14 March 2024. https://niopa.qub.ac.uk/bitstream/NIOPA/15973/1/Legacy%20Bill%20FINAL.pdf.

Portelli, Alessandro. 1981. 'The peculiarities of oral history'. *History Workshop Journal* 12(1): 96–107.

Roulston, Fearghus. 2017. 'Oral history and pluralizing the past in post-conflict Northern Ireland'. *Oral History Forum d'historie orale. Special Issue on Oral History and Religion* 37: 1–24. https://www.oralhistoryforum.ca/index.php/ohf/article/view/643

Smith, Laurajane. 2006. *The Uses of Heritage*. London: Routledge.

Stoler, Ann Laura. 2002. 'Colonial archives and the acts of governance'. *Archival Science* 2: 87–109.

Stoler, Ann Laura. 2010. 'Archival dis-ease: Thinking through colonial ontologies'. *Communication and Critical/Cultural Studies* 7(2): 215–19.

Swain, Ellen D. 2003. 'Oral history in the archives: Its documentary role in the twenty-first century'. *The American Archivist* 66(1): 139–58.

Taylor, Lisa Karen. 2018. 'Pedagogies of remembrance and "doing critical heritage" in the teaching of history: Countermemorializing Canada 150 with future teachers'. *Journal of Canadian Studies* 52(1): 217–48.

Viggiani, Elisabetta. 2014. *Talking Stones: The politics of memorialisation in post-conflict Northern Ireland*. Oxford: Berghahn Books.

Wright, Patrick. 1985. *On Living in an Old Country*. Oxford: Oxford University Press.

Zemon Davis, Natalie. 2010. *Passion for History: Conversations with Denis Crouzet*. Philadelphia, PA: Penn State University Press.

6 On commemorating

Leticia Zuppardi

In 2006, parts of the Nazi-era battleship *Graf Spee* were recovered from the bay of Montevideo, Uruguay, on the Río de la Plata. It had been intentionally sunk here by order of its captain after the Battle of the Río de la Plata – the first naval battle between English and German ships during World War II and the only one that took place in the South Atlantic – on 13 December 1939. For 67 years, remnants of the ship remained undisturbed until 2006, when it was partially recovered. The piece of the warship that was extracted was a massive bronze sculpture of an eagle standing over 2.35 metres tall and weighing over 300 kilograms. Below its impressively spread wings, the eagle grips the infamous Nazi party symbol, a swastika, with its claws.

As news of the object was circulated in the media, the swastika was covered with a cloth since the image could raise uncomfortable feelings. Nevertheless, the eagle was briefly displayed at a hotel in Montevideo before being transferred to a warehouse under the custody of the Uruguayan navy following a public, local and transnational pushback. What followed was a legal, diplomatic and social dispute surrounding the value of a historical object thrust into a familiar battleground for many monuments across the world. The private company responsible for the underwater rescue sought repayment in the form of an auction that could have attracted Nazi sympathisers. On its side, the Uruguayan government claimed the proprietary rights of the eagle. Ultimately, a legal process awarded ownership of the object to the Uruguayan state, who then proposed smelting the eagle in order to transform it into a dove, a monument to peace and unity. A renowned Uruguayan artist, Pablo Atchugarry, was commissioned to recast the eagle and perform this radical transmutation.

Although this idea received some support when announced, the predominant reaction was that of outrage. Private individuals, associations and prominent figures from various fields, locally and internationally, declared their opposition to this measure. As a result, this proposal was discarded, and the eagle of the *Graf Spee* has remained in storage since then. As monuments are made and unmade across the world, rarely do we witness such a failed birthing of a new monument, raising the question of why there has been so much resistance to understanding a monument's destruction, modification or even failed creation as a part of its archival life.

Throughout the late twentieth and early twenty-first centuries, the fate of monuments has become a defining narrative in our cultural landscape. Physical landmarks that once influenced our perception of urban spaces more conspicuously are now leading the way in the process of challenging conventional historical narratives. It is clear now that monuments can also be a source of discomfort, spark strong emotions and lead to disputes resulting in relocation or alterations, either through official channels or through the actions of communities and individuals. As our awareness of the negative impacts of colonialism, ethnocentrism, patriarchal mindsets, racism and heteronormativity on our society grows, resistance to symbols of these systems will likely continue to increase. This means that heritage practitioners and scholars need to be better prepared to address the challenges related to monument destruction.

The strong emotional response to destroying a historical object, in this case through the creation of a new monument, suggests a lack of awareness of how these objects operate as archives and within a complex network of archives – the historical documents produced during its creation, existence and eventual destruction. While the dove born out of the *Graf Spee* never materialised, its aspirations for embodying certain values for the national identity of Uruguay live on in discussions and legislative texts. The materialisation of this project would have generated documents ranging from estimates to invoices and plans. The inauguration of the dove would have brought along speeches, press releases and official photographic records, followed by a lifetime of posts on social media and countless marks in the memory of individuals who inhabit those spaces. The monument's life could also accumulate graffiti, vandalism, relocation and total destruction. In the end, a monument may continue to exist regardless of its physicality.

Approaches in critical archival studies can provide a stimulating perspective to understand and capture the complex archival web associated with reframing monuments as archives. The result of applying critical theory to archival studies has been advanced by Caswell, Punzalan and Sangwand (2017), who characterise critical archival studies as a set of approaches that broaden the scope of the archival field beyond a practice-focused internal orientation. Instead, this approach seeks to build a critical perspective and attitude regarding the role of archives in the production of knowledge and different kinds of narratives, as well as the construction of identities. In this way, critical archival studies aim to transform archival practice and society's attitudes to archiving in general.

Transcending the idea of a monument as something eternally carved in stone to conceptualise it instead as something alive and dynamic in the collective memory does not deter from its ability to be preserved, disseminated and made available to the public through archival sources produced along its life history. It is also a productive way to negotiate the impact of monumental losses. Such a holistic and organic view allows us to approach the monument as a piece of a larger story related to other components and to disentangle the process of commemoration from the monument itself. Bringing complexity and depth to our understanding of how we handle commemoration practices from the past and recent history when memorials are objects of destruction, relocation and reinterpretation becomes not only exciting and thought-provoking but also crucial for reconsidering the role of commemoration in the study of heritage value.

REFERENCES AND RESOURCES

Caswell, Michelle. 2017. 'Owning critical archival studies: A plea'. *UCLA*. https://escholarship.org/uc/item/75x090df

Caswell, Michelle, Ricardo Punzalan and T-Kay Sangwand. 2017. 'Critical archival studies: An introduction'. *Journal of Critical Library and Information Studies* 1(2): 1–8.

7 Collections and collecting

Alice Stevenson

DESCRIPTION AND HISTORIOGRAPHY

Collections are formed in a variety of contexts, for personal, professional and institutional reasons. The focus of this chapter is the latter: museums and archives relating to archaeology and anthropology. These, like all collections, were generated at different times, in different contexts and therefore now not only preserve the objects/assemblages themselves but also a way of seeing and governing the world.

Since their emergence in the mid-nineteenth century, archaeology and anthropology have had their disciplinary identities most clearly articulated vis-à-vis 'the field' (Brinitzer and Benson 2022). Constructing knowledge in this model is traditionally assumed to occur at a physical distance from institutions – making discoveries within excavation trenches or documenting ethnographic information within communities, for instance. Such encounters themselves generated new forms of material heritage, which was recognised in the nineteenth and early twentieth century as a 'material anthropology' (Gosden and Larson 2007, 121–46) that gave objects a primary role in Victorian perceptions of the world. The status and potential of these artefacts were then further transformed as they travelled from the field to what Bruno Latour (1987) termed 'centres of calculation', where they were subsumed within larger collections that formed the evidential basis for knowledge claims in the metropole.

Following anthropology's 'crisis of representation' in the mid-1980s, these 'centres of calculation' – museums, universities, archives and libraries – were reinvigorated as active field sites in their own right. Researchers now sought to use collections for purposes quite different from those who established them. This has involved reading archives 'along the grain' (Stoler 2010), interrogating the histories and agencies behind their accumulation (e.g. Byrne et al. 2011), examining their role in the production of cultural representations (Moser 2010) and collaborating with source communities on their futures (Thorner 2022). This realignment of heritage values has necessitated a shift from prioritising objects as evidence in and of themselves to examining their institutional framings and histories. This recognises the multifaceted nature of collections, from finds and specimens to photographs, diaries, letters, replicas and models, together with their documentation in catalogues, registers, labels and databases.

In practice, therefore, navigating collections is a recursive process of working between object and archive, tracking their movements, relationships with people and other artefacts, and their shifting statuses over time. Prominent frameworks that have been adopted to this end include object biographies and actor–network theory. The former has been embraced within the museum sector as its narrative potential is seen to facilitate not only research but also public communication. The latter has principally been taken more as a general metaphor for the wider circulation of collections rather than a full adoption of Latour's theorisation on the agencies of things ('actants'). A theoretical genealogy for such approaches lies in anthropologist Arun Appadurai's (1986) ideas regarding 'things-in-motion' and Igor Kopytoff's (1986) 'life histories' models (e.g. Gosden and Marshall 1999; Alberti 2005), themselves inheritors of Malinowski (1922) and Mauss's (1925) insights on 'gift-giving'. Collectively, these works emphasise how objects and people mutually gain value and status relative to each other through object circulation. For instance, a donation to a collection may secure for the donor cultural esteem, while the artefact retains an identity relative to the donor (e.g. the Elgin Marbles).

While the biographical approach has been useful, it implies a linear narrative, from 'birth' to 'death', when in reality artefact mobility is more complex (Hahn and Weiss 2013). To better reflect this the idea of 'itineraries' has been offered (Joyce and Gillespie 2015).

Others have rejected biographical models altogether as inappropriate for collections research, retaining as they do the kernels of 'gifting' theories when collections often embody the opposite – violence and dispossession (Hicks 2020). These histories, Hicks argues, are 'stifled' by the notion of life histories, which through incremental recontextualisation move away from and obscure earlier moments. Such rejection may be premature. Geismar (2021) has written in their defence, arguing that biographies 'empower and create space for voices from outside the institution'. Taking Geismar's point further, a more productive way of approaching collections histories is to consider their potential to be 'multidirectional'. This term references historian Michael Rothberg's (2014) contention that rather than different histories competing with each other, they can work 'productively through negotiation, cross-referencing, and borrowing' so that 'collective memories of seemingly distinct histories are not easily separable from each other but emerge dialogically' (Rothberg 2014, 176). There can be a hundred histories of a hundred worlds in one object (Brusius, Stevenson and Das 2019).

Related to, but more complex than, object biographies is actor–network theory (ANT), again derived from Latour, which has encouraged viewing collections as social assemblages (Byrne et al. 2011). Gosden and Larson (2007), for instance, conducted an extended case study of the Pitt Rivers Museum, quantitatively and qualitatively analysing the museum's database and archives to chart the history of personal and professional relations forged through collecting. In their resulting 'relational museum' model it was not only people that collected objects; objects also collected people. Artefacts thereby come to stand for the networks that formed them, and collections are conceived of as congealed masses of relations between local antiquarians, travellers, dealers, private collectors and museums. Quantitative methods can be employed to capture and visualise these networks, such as employing computer-generated network diagrams that statistically map routes taken by objects into centres of calculation (Larson, Petch and Zeitlyn 2007), although these can be criticised for treating all connections as being of equal importance. Key, however, to any quantitative analysis is historical contextualisation to disclose the social or political conditions that facilitated, encouraged or constrained particular interests.

There are several issues with commencing analysis from centres of calculation. One is that it focuses attention almost exclusively on prominent individuals or institutions at the end of collection chains, while the intermediaries that made such collections and claims to knowledge possible, such as 'invisible technicians' (Shapin 1989), are rarely as apparent within archival records. Attitudes to race, class and gender all conspire to render individual roles opaque in documentation. A second issue is the assumption that centres of calculation exist only in colonial facilities, although networks extended throughout and beyond empires. While these may have engaged with and responded to foreign encounters, they were not always set up with the goal of replicating knowledge in Eurocentric ways, as Achim (2017) has highlighted for Latin American collections. The association of objects with their Indigenous excavators is a further case in point, with the names of 'hidden hands' responsible for field retrieval rarely travelling with artefacts (Quirke 2010). A third concern is that these models, while theoretically acknowledging the relationships between people and things, in execution have resulted in studies that focus more on the former. Yet as Svanberg (2015) has cautioned, collections, and the systems they create and consolidate, have their own agency that structure the institutions they are in, meaning that the infrastructures collections are embedded in require equal consideration alongside historical actors and objects, for example systems of classification (see below) and display strategies.

A final concern with ANT is the weight of scholarship given to colonial collecting and their collectors, which although vital for transparency and redress does then recentre those historical encounters at the expense of alternative departure points that seek to generate other heritage values such as those relating to contemporary identities, ritual practice or revitalisation (e.g. Peers 2013; Macdonald, Lidchi and von Oswald 2017). Collections here have potential for forging new types of social relations and meanings, what have been termed 'contact zones' in which 'people geographically and historically separated come into contact with each other and establish ongoing relations' (Clifford 1997, 192). The idea of the contact zone is a popular frame for institutions seeking to bring previously marginalised voices into dialogue with collections, but too often this still privileges the site of the museum as the primary authority (Boast 2011). How historic collections might operate, benefit and have significance outside of institutions for source communities (Peers and Brown 2003; Abd el-Gawad and Stevenson 2021), to tell histories of relevance to them on their own terms, is a pressing issue outside of the scope of this chapter. Suffice to say that the intersection of heritage studies with collections must be cognisant of narrative cues, institutional biases and positionalities in how collections are framed and investigated (see 'Teaching' below).

PRAXIS

The shifting values of collections and their constituent parts, as well as the multiple agencies associated with them, is thrown into relief during their circulation (Driver, Nesbitt and Cornish 2021). The distribution of archaeological finds from British excavations in Egypt can serve as an example (Stevenson, Libonati and Williams 2016; Stevenson 2019). Between 1880 and 1980, more than 350 institutions in 27 countries across five continents benefitted from a colonial system of partage. This practice permitted foreign-led archaeological projects to share the finds from fieldwork with the authorities in Cairo and was adopted by other countries working in Egypt and elsewhere. Partage helped archaeological organisations leverage funding for their excavations from museums, with the promise of material returns that would expand institutional collections.

The partage system was negotiated on the basis that some finds were not required in Egypt as they were construed as duplicates or else uninteresting specimens. Thus, while patrimony laws did exist in Egypt from the early nineteenth century, they primarily focused upon the monumental, the inscribed or the unique (Colla 2005), leaving space for the negotiation of material falling outside of these categories. The situation highlights the contingencies of object value, with decisions on what to collect from archaeological sites made relative to collections in Cairo and centres of calculation abroad. What were considered duplicates in the former context were reappraised as unique and valuable in the latter, while their significance was further constructed through associations with particular individuals such as famous excavators or wealthy donors and elevated in relation to institutional values (be those religious, scholarly or artistic). Given that hundreds of thousands of artefacts were dispersed in this process, in practice it is rare to be able to map out the biography of individual items (Joy 2009). Working laterally across sources, however, can permit a broader picture of the social, political or economic contexts that facilitated the movement of material in general.

A 5,000-year-old pottery vessel in the Petrie Museum of Egyptian Archaeology, London, serves as an example of the multitude of histories and people implicated in its collection. The vessel is of a type known as 'Black-Topped pottery' (B-ware), a classification established by English archaeologist Flinders Petrie in the late 1890s as a foundational step in his development of 'seriation' (the relative ordering of pottery deemed to be indicative of a chronological sequence). It is a method for which Petrie is famous, with collections of such objects frequently tied to this narrative of Victorian scientific advancement. However, this specific vessel bears clues that allow biographies to be taken in different directions. On the rim, inked upon a layer of lacquer, is the code 'UC5699', which is an accession (registration) number that identifies the object as an official part of the Petrie Museum collection, and which extends it into an ecosystem of related historical documentation including accession registers, index cards and databases. The record for UC5699 highlights other nodes in the collection's history such as the site of its excavation – the cemetery of Naqada, tomb 1817. It is this latter number that is written directly on the base of the vessel and tethers it to other archival records, including those referred to as the 'Petrie notebooks' that contain plans of excavated graves permitting inferences on burial practices and agencies in the fourth millennium BC. The notebooks' title is a misnomer, however, as few were written by Petrie. The document in which burial 1817 is recorded instead bears the name 'Hugh Price', one of several volunteers that joined Petrie that season. His sketch of grave 1817 is annotated with numerous labels, including a third name, Ali Redwan, the Egyptian workman who cleared the tomb.

What these records further reveal is that this vessel was one of dozens recovered from grave 1817. Further documents in the Petrie Museum list other institutions that received objects from Naqada, each allocated on the basis of how much funding had been supplied to Petrie, much of it through donations from private citizens (often wealthy industrialists) keen to see their own cultural capital cemented through philanthropic means for their local institutions. Each was absorbed into different types of collections, institutions that might emphasise art or ethnography as opposed to archaeology, and which were underpinned by alternative institutional structures, histories and individuals who shaped the meanings of objects in particular ways, localising global histories. There was not a singular fascination with the land of the pharaohs; rather, these objects were much more malleable and integrated within a range of other agendas. Notably, not all of the organisations listed in such records necessarily still have the allocated artefacts today. Collections are never static, so while histories of collection frequently focus on accumulation, removals and rationalisation are equally part of institutional histories (Stevenson 2019, 181–216). Duplicates, for example, could be identified and sent to other organisations (Nichols 2016). Ongoing circulation may also occur through means of reproduction (e.g. plaster casts), an alternative technology of collecting that permitted numerous institutions to share in the 'composite biography' (Foster and Jones 2020) of a single artefact, highlighting parallel but contingent histories.

TEACHING

Collections work affords opportunities for a range of assignment types (e.g. portfolios, exhibition reviews or reports) beyond the traditional essay. In the context of museums, object-based learning can be a more active mode of education leading to a fresh remobilisation of historic collections for higher education programmes (Chatterjee and Hannan 2015). However, much of that literature focuses on direct, isolated material inference and sensorial engagement by the viewer or handler, but collections work additionally requires contextualisation with a range of related documentation and a sensitivity towards other culturally situated means of knowing (Hodge 2018). For these reasons such assessments can be daunting for students who, while confident in engaging with scholarship, may be far less confident in evaluating the primary evidence upon which this is based, a divide noted by others seeking to apply theory to practice (Adams 2015). The object biography model, although helpful for unfurling complex histories, may need to be broken down into constituent parts to look at discrete 'collection events', be they the moment of field collection, the actions of museum acquisition and cataloguing, through to present display or other collection uses. It is not always possible to pinpoint exactly where or when an object was found or entered a museum. Documentation may be limited. In these situations, it is helpful to look for comparative examples and broader-level histories that characterise the general period and socio-political conditions under which an object may have been removed. For instance, what cultural heritage laws were in place? What sort of language was used at that time? Finding similar objects in other collections can provide parallel histories that can be informative. This is where portfolio work (e.g. Paulson, Paulson and Meyer 1991) with different types of exercises and different styles of writing can be helpful, as well as accommodating Indigenous research methods should that be appropriate (Bruhac 2020).

In these contexts, students may need help to navigate and critically understand sources of information that coalesce around and inform objects, be they historical literature, auction catalogues, museum databases or associated archives, so as to identify biases, gaps or inaccuracies. This includes bringing critical attention to the infrastructures that have conditioned the sorts of information collected about objects. Greene (2016), for instance, points to the replication of nineteenth-century modes of colonial information organisation that are passed from original catalogues through to card indexes, and into computer databases and online search engines. Therefore, taking time to examine the biases of and language used in collections documentation (Turner 2016), as well as the historical contexts in which these were produced, is valuable. When were these records produced? Whose value systems do those categories and associated information work for? To this end, it is worth taking time to explore the different types of object database fields associated with a record, together with undertaking and evaluating online catalogue searches, and experimenting in creating object records to encourage critical thinking around words or terms that allow information retrieval, as well as some of the challenges to their use. Students can be encouraged to examine not just the material properties of objects but also markings or labels upon them. Consider, for instance, that artefacts may be catalogued and documented for different purposes indicative of alternative valuation systems and points in their history. For example, markings on objects may have been applied by field collectors to denote context, date or affiliation; commercial dealers to indicate price, lot or value; private collectors to assimilate acquisitions within personal assemblages; or by museum staff to assign an object to a particular collection, subcollection or museum department. One impediment is that such work is often dependent upon access to relevant records and may require considerable preparation and dialogue with museum professionals.

Finally, in framing such classes it is important to note at the outset that although the encounter with collections and their narratives may be an intellectually stimulating experience, for those historically marginalised or racialised by institutional practices it may be emotional, indeed distressing. Engagement with collections may negatively impact those with lived experience of coloniality, discrimination or trauma, as Jilda Andrews (2017), a Yuwaalaraay scholar, notes for Indigenous agents confronting collections. Similarly, Temi Odumosu (2020) asks researchers to question the extent to which institutions take seriously non-European perspectives on looking at, or engaging with, materials. Teaching with and learning from collections therefore needs to consider researchers' positionalities and reflect upon who benefits from collections work, how this is framed and how research results might be reincorporated back within institutional memory. Here it is not just collections histories that might be considered in class discussion or assessment, but the potentials for future intellectual, creative or restorative engagements.

This chapter has considered how collections can be interrogated in the twenty-first century for different types of heritage values relating to the peoples and places implicated in their formation and legacies. Heritage studies can draw out these values to varying degrees using a range of methods. This entails approaching collections as multiply constituted, paying attention not just to their material facts and affects but also to their relational properties within an ecosystem of archival locations, institutional framings and associated people.

REFERENCES AND RESOURCES

Abd el-Gawad, Heba and Alice Stevenson. 2021. 'Egypt's dispersed heritage: Using comic art for multidirectional storytelling'. *Journal of Social Archaeology* 21(1): 121–45.

Achim, Miruna. 2017. *From Idols to Antiquity: Forging the National Museum of Mexico*. Lincoln, NE: University of Nebraska Press.

Adams, Kathleen M. 2015. 'Back to the future? Emergent visons for object-based teaching in and beyond the classroom'. *Museum Anthropology* 38(2): 88–95.

Alberti, Samuel. 2005. 'Objects and the museum'. *Isis* 96(4): 559–71.

Andrews, Jilda. 2017. 'Indigenous perspectives on museum collections'. *Artlink* 37(2): 88–91.

Appadurai, Arjun. 1986. 'Introduction: commodities and the politics of value'. In *The Social Life of Things: Commodities in cultural perspective*, edited by Arjun Appadurai, 3–63. Cambridge: Cambridge University Press.

Boast, Robin. 2011. 'Neo-colonial collaboration: museum as contact zone revisited'. *Museum Anthropology* 34(1): 56–70.

Brinitzer, Cameron and Etienne Benson. 2022. 'Introduction: What is a field? Transformations in fields, fieldwork, and field sciences since the mid-twentieth century'. *Isis* 113(1).

Bruhac, Margaret. 2020. 'Restorative research in the Penn Museum collection'. *Penn Today* blog, 8 April. Accessed 11 March 2024. https://penntoday.upenn.edu/news/canada-naskapi-nation-visit-penn-museum-native-american-collection.

Brusius, Mirjam, Alice Stevenson and Subhadra Das. 2019. '100 histories of 100 worlds in one object: An interview with Mirjam Brusius, Subhadra Das and Alice Stevenson'. *TRAFO – Blog for Transregional Research*, 5 December. Accessed 11 March 2024. https://trafo.hypotheses.org/20851.

Byrne, Sarah, Anne Clarke, Rodney Harrison and Robin Torrence. 2011. 'Networks, agents and objects: Frameworks for unpacking museum collections'. In *Unpacking the Collection: Networks of material and social agency in the museum*, edited by Sarah Byrne, Anne Clarke, Rodney Harrison and Robin Torrence, 3–26. New York: Springer.

Chatterjee, Helen and Hannan, Leonie (eds) 2015. *Engaging the Senses: Object-based learning in higher education*. London: Routledge.

Clifford, James. 1997. 'Museums as contact zones'. In *Routes: Travel and translation in the late twentieth century*, edited by James Clifford, 188–219. Cambridge, MA: Harvard University Press.

Colla, Elliott. 2005. 'Anxious advocacy: The novel and the law in Egypt'. *Public Culture* 17(3): 417–43.

Dalal-Clayton, Anjalie and Ananda Rutherford. 2022. 'Against a new orthodoxy: decolonised 'objectivity' in the cataloguing and description of artworks'. *Paul Mellon Centre Photographic Archive*.Accessed 11 March 2024. https://photoarchive.paul-mellon-centre.ac.uk/groups/against-a-new-orthodoxy.

Das, Subhadra and Miranda Lowe. 2019. 'Nature read in black and white: Decolonial approaches to interpreting natural history collections'. *Journal of Natural Science Collections* 6: 4–14.

Driver, Felix, Mark Nesbitt and Caroline Cornish (eds) 2021. *Mobile Museums: Collections in circulation*. London: UCL Press.

Edwards, Elizabeth and Christopher Morton. 2015. 'Between art and information: Towards a collecting history of photographs'. In *Photographs, Museums, Collections: Between art and information*, edited by Elizabeth Edwards and Christopher Morton, 3–23. London: Bloomsbury Academic.

Foster, Sally and Siân Jones. 2020. *My Life as a Replica: St. John's Cross, Iona*. Oxford: Windgather Press.

Geismar, Haidy. 2018. *Museum Object Lessons for the Digital Age*. London: UCL Press.

Geismar, Haidy. 2021. 'In defence of the object biography'. *British Art Studies* 19.

Gosden, Chris and Marshall, Yvonne 1999. 'The cultural biography of things'. *World Archaeology* 31(2): 169–78.

Gosden, Chris and Frances Larson. 2007. *Knowing Things: Exploring the collections of the Pitt Rivers Museum 1884–1945*. Oxford: Oxford University Press.

Greene, Candace. 2016. 'Material connections: "The Smithsonian Effect" in anthropological cataloguing'. *Museum Anthropology* 39(2): 147–62.

Hahn, Hans P. and Hadas Weiss. 2013. 'Introduction: Biographies, travels and itineraries of things'. In *Mobility, Meaning and Transformations of Things: Shifting contexts of material culture through time and space*, edited by Hans P. Hahn and Hadas Weiss, 1–14. Oxford: Oxbow.

Hicks, Dan. 2020. 'Necrography: Death-writing in the colonial museum'. *British Art Studies* 19.

Hodge, Christina J. 2018. 'Decolonizing collection-based learning: Experiential observation as an interdisciplinary framework for object study'. *Museum Anthropology* 41(2): 142–58.

Jones, Mike. 2021. *Artefacts, Archives, and Documentation in the Relational Museum*. London: Routledge.

Joy, Jody. 2009. 'Reinvigorating object biography: Reproducing the drama of object lives'. *World Archaeology* 41(4): 540–56.

Joyce, Rosemary and Susan D. Gillespie (eds) 2015. *Things in Motion: Object itineraries in anthropological practice*. Santa Fe, NM: SAR Press.

Kopytoff, Igor. 1986. 'The cultural biography of things: Commoditization as process'. In *The Social Life of Things: Commodities in cultural perspective*, edited by Arjun Appadurai, 64–91. Cambridge: Cambridge University Press.

Larson, Frances, Alison Petch and David Zeitlyn. 2007. 'Social networks and the creation of the Pitt Rivers Museum'. *Journal of Material Culture* 12(3): 211–39.

Latour, Bruno. 1987. *Science in Action: How to follow scientists and engineers through society*. Cambridge, MA: Harvard University Press.

Macdonald, Sharon, Henrietta Lidchi and Margareta von Oswald. 2017. 'Engaging anthropological legacies toward cosmo-optimistic futures?' *Museum Worlds* 5: 95–107.

Malinowski, Bronisław. 1922. *Argonauts of the Western Pacific*. London: Routledge.

Mauss, Marcel. 1966 [1925]. *The Gift: Forms and functions of exchange in archaic societies*. London: Cohen and West.

Morphy, Howard. 2015. 'The displaced local: Multiple agency in the building of museums ethnographic collections'. In *The International Handbook of Museum Studies: Museum theory*, edited by Kylie Message and Andrea Witcomb, 365–86. Chichester: Wiley-Blackwell.

Moser, Stephanie. 2010. 'The devil is in the detail: Museum displays and the creation of knowledge'. *Museum Anthropology* 33(1): 22–32.

Nichols, Catherine A. 2016. 'Exchanging anthropological duplicates at the Smithsonian Institute'. *Museum Anthropology* 39(2): 130–46.

Odumosu, Temi. 2020. 'The crying child: On colonial archives, digitization, and ethics of care in the cultural commons'. *Cultural Anthropology* 61(s22): 289–302.

Paulson, F. Leon, Pearl R. Paulson and Carol A. Meyer. 1991. 'What makes a portfolio a portfolio?' *Educational Leadership* 48: 60–4.

Peers, Laura. 2013. 'Ceremonies of renewal: Visits, relationships and healing in the museum space'. *Museum Worlds* 1(1): 136–52.

Peers, Laura and Alison Brown (eds) 2003. 'Introduction'. In *Museums and Source Communities*, 1–16. London: Routledge.

Quirke, Stephen. 2010. *Hidden Hands: Egyptian workforces in Petrie excavation archives, 1880–1924*. London: Duckworth.

Rothberg, Michael. 2014. 'Multidirectional memory'. *Témoigner: Entre histoire et mémoire* 119.

Shapin, Steven. 1989. 'The invisible technician'. *American Scientist* 77(6): 554–63.

Stevenson, Alice. 2019. *Scattered Finds: Archaeology, Egyptology, and museums*. London: UCL Press.

Stevenson, Alice, Emma Libonati and Alice Williams. 2016. '"A selection of minor antiquities": A multi-sited view on collections from excavations in Egypt'. *World Archaeology* 48(2): 282–95.

Stoler, Ann L. 2010. *Along the Archival Grain: Epistemic anxieties and colonial common sense*. Princeton, NJ: Princeton University Press.

Svanberg, Fredrik. 2015. 'The world as collected; Or the museum collections as situated materialities'. In *The International Handbooks of Museum Studies: Museum theories*, edited by Andrea Witcomb and Kylie Message, 389–416. London: Wiley-Blackwell.

Thorner, Sabra G. 2022. 'Being called to action: Contemporary museum ethnographies'. *Museum Anthropology* 45(1): 3–14.

Turner, Hannah. 2016. 'Critical histories of museum catalogues'. *Museum Anthropology* 29(2): 102–10.

8 On not (just) repatriating

Elizabeth Marlowe

In the US, it used to be common for antiquities collectors or their heirs to donate their holdings to museums in exchange for tax relief. But in 2008, the Association of Art Museum Directors (AAMD) and the American Alliance of Museums (AAM), the two leading professional organisations, issued guidelines urging member institutions to refuse donations of antiquities that don't comply with the 1970 UNESCO Convention (AAMD 2008). Archaeology and heritage protection organisations seeking to reduce the incidence of looting had been advocating for such a policy for decades. Since looting occurs to meet the demand of collectors, a key strategy to stop future looting has been to disincentivise collecting. By refusing to accept donations of possibly looted artworks, museums deny collectors both the tax breaks and the social capital that normally come with that particular form of charity.

There is no doubt that this strict policy has forced the collecting community to confront the reality of the connection between collecting and looting. But it also raises a question: what is happening to all the antiquities that private collectors purchased after 1970? When those people pass away or decide they no longer want to keep their collections, where are the artefacts going? Do those of us interested in the protection of archaeological heritage, those who pushed museums to adopt the policy they finally adopted in 2008, have any duty of care to already-looted, privately owned antiquities? Should we be concerned about their preservation? Should a goal be to prevent them from returning to – and thereby refuelling – the market?

A related question is: can any heritage value be extracted from such objects and collections? If the context of their archaeological discovery is doomed to remain forever unknown to us, are there other ways of knowing or valorising them – other networks of human relations within which they can be contextualised? Other nodes along their 'object itineraries' (Bauer 2019) that are worth examining? Finally, is there any way to explore these topics for privately owned, poorly provenanced artefacts without increasing their market value or excusing the behaviour of the collectors who purchased them (Brodie 2011)?

One approach to these interconnected problems has been to advocate for the immediate repatriation of all poorly documented antiquities and artefacts to the countries from which they were likely looted. For example, there was much favourable press coverage about an American man, John Gomperts, who read a newspaper article about looting and repatriation and realised that artefacts he'd inherited from his grandmother 'could have come from illicit excavations because they have no collecting history' (Alberge 2022). Eager to do the right thing, he contacted Christos Tsirogiannis, the expert in antiquities trafficking cited in the article. Based on the photographs Gomperts sent him, Tsirogiannis identified the artefacts as a pair of seventh-century Cypriot vases, fourth-century south Italian vases and a stone relief depicting the followers of Buddha, from the third or second century BC. Tsirogiannis advised him to wrap the artefacts up carefully and deliver them to the appropriate Washington DC embassies. Gomperts followed his advice. 'The countries showed their appreciation with notes of thanks to Gomperts and Tsirogiannis', according to an article in *The Guardian* (Alberge 2022).

I am not persuaded that this is the optimum solution to the conundrum of what to do with looted antiquities. I believe owners – whether individuals like Gomperts or public museums – have a responsibility to ensure a full account of how they came to possess looted artefacts. We will never understand how to disrupt trafficking networks without researching how they work. Nor will we understand the complex ways in which archaeological artefacts accrue heritage value and engender social relations without exploring who has owned them and why. In the case of Gomperts, an opportunity may have been missed to dig deeper into the story of his German-Dutch grandmother, Gisela Schneider-Herrman, who had worked on digs in the mid-twentieth century, donated other antiquities to the Rijksmuseum van Outheyden (the Dutch National Antiquities Museum) and published on ancient ceramics. Maybe something in these sources or the Outheyden archives would reveal more about the provenance of her American collection. Maybe an oral history project with Gomperts and his relatives might have revealed when and how and why this subset of her collection came to the US. While the archaeological find-spot of these antiquities may not be recoverable, it's possible that other chapters in their 'object biographies' or 'itineraries' might be. What was the relationship between these artefacts and the ones she excavated? Why were some pieces in her collection given to a museum and others kept in the family? With research, archaeologically undocumented artefacts can teach us about the history of collecting, looting, the valuation of antiquities, shifting ethical norms and other modern topics.

University museums would be particularly well positioned and well equipped to do this work, if the 2008 AAM and Association of Academic Museums and Galleries (AAMG) guidelines were revised to allow them to accept donations of unprovenanced objects for the purpose of conducting provenance research and determining the most appropriate long-term home for them. As long as the artefacts were already donated to the museum before the research began, there would be no risk of increasing their market value. Courses and exhibits addressing difficult, unflattering or sordid histories – what we might call 'negative heritage' (Meskell 2002; Rico 2008) would be protected by the principle of academic freedom. Faculty in a range of disciplines – such as anthropology, religion, chemistry, history, art history, geography, sociology – could lend their expertise. Students could be trained in the methods of provenance research (including oral history with collectors), which is certain to be a growing field in coming years. If an identified source country deemed repatriation to be appropriate, university museums could hand over the objects without any perception of compromising their mission. Furthermore, the ties forged between the university and cultural officials, scholars and curators in the source country could serve as the basis for ongoing relationships, possibly allowing student and/or faculty exchanges and continuing research collaborations.

An organisation such as the Association of Academic Museums and Galleries could perhaps oversee these donations of private collections to university museums to ensure that various legal and ethical parameters are met (Marlowe 2022). In this way, repatriation could be part of a larger story that includes both pre-repatriation research and ongoing, post-repatriation relationships. Researching and telling these stories is not only part of our duty of care to these objects; it is also likely, through education, to reduce future looting.

REFERENCES AND RESOURCES

Alberge, Dalya. 2022. 'Man repatriates 19 antiquities after reading Guardian article'. *The Guardian*, 11 November.

Association of Art Museum Directors (AAMD). 2008. 'New acquisitions of archaeological material and works of ancient art'. Accessed 11 March 2024. https://aamd.org/object-registry/new-acquisitions-of-archaeological-material-and-works-of-ancient-art/more-info.

Bauer, Alexander. 2019. 'Itinerant objects'. *Annual Review of Anthropology* 49: 335–52.

Brodie, Neil. 2011. 'Congenial bedfellows? The Academy and the antiquities trade'. *Journal of Contemporary Criminal Justice* 27: 408–37.

Marlowe, Elizabeth. 2022. '"Responsible stewards" of classical antiquities? The Society for American Archaeology's "Statement on Collaboration" and Non-American material culture'. *Advances in Archaeological Practice* 10: 249–57.

Meskell, Lynn. 2002. 'Negative heritage and past mastering in archaeology'. *Anthropological Quarterly* 75: 557–74.

Rico, Trinidad. 2008. 'Negative heritage: The place of conflict in world heritage'. *Conservation and Management of Archaeological Sites* 10: 344–52.

9 Institutions and governance

Christina Luke

DESCRIPTION AND HISTORIOGRAPHY

An intellectual exercise at its core, engaging with processes of (re)learning and (re)remembering, the concern with governance in the world of heritage pivots around the key question of *what* is chosen at any given time to represent desired pasts. We can therefore consider heritage as both a thing being governed (subject to regulation, safeguarding and promotion) and also a platform for enabling (or sometimes disabling) governance. Governance refers not only to how nation-states provide for and make demands of their citizens (however these are defined), but also to international forms of statecraft through economic, military and diplomatic interventions – these last constituting one of the major forces behind global heritage management and presentation. These practices are enacted through institutions that operate across multiple scales: global intergovernmental organisations (e.g. the UN and its agencies, the World Bank, the New Development Bank); state departments, parastatal entities and independent agencies authorised or sponsored by central governments (e.g. USAID); regional multilateral organisations (e.g. the European Union, the Gulf Cooperation Council); and locally focused and 'grassroots' groups. The configuration of these entities varies in space and time, across forms of government (including where these are highly contested, e.g. Palestine, Somaliland) and in situations where governance has been dramatically transformed through political conflict or restructuring within 'development' programmes. To that end, development agencies can and have served as agents of governance by imposing conditions on resources donated, loaned or otherwise invested in recipient nations. While the concept of global heritage originated as a transnational one, the interests of the nation-state and subnational entities are ultimately 'critical to cultural heritage oversight', producing tensions when these interests conflict with those elsewhere in the wider web of international and diplomatic relations (Kersel and Luke 2015, 74).

The making of global heritage governance is frequently presented through the institutionalisation of heritage concerns by the United Nations Educational and Scientific Organization (UNESCO), an entity that emerged in 1946 with great fan-fare and promise (Betts and Ross 2015). From this point on, there has been a steady growth in institutions and instruments. First, a concern with heritage in conflict was addressed by an international community in the 1954 Convention for the Protection of Cultural Property in the Event of Armed Conflict and then more broadly applied to the problem of plunder through the 1970 Convention on the Means of Prohibiting and Preventing the Illicit Import, Export and Transfer of Ownership of Cultural Property (Luke and Kersel 2013; Gerstenblith 2014, 2008). In this era of heritage internationalism, principles underpinning intervention and training were set forth in the 1964 Venice Charter, supporting and standardising the internationalism of salvage campaigns along the Nile (Betts 2015). Finally, UNESCO's crowning finale was the 1972 Convention Concerning the Protection of World Cultural and Natural Heritage (Cleere 2011; Meskell 2018). Utopian visions of peace, prosperity and mutual understanding infused the rhetoric of these benchmark doctrinal documents and charted a new era for governing heritage from the position of a united, global platform.

Over the last 40 years, scholarship has peeled back the layers of these intentions to reveal cracks in the diplomatic armour that sustained such a system of governance, giving rise to a study of heritage that is deeply concerned with international, regional and local politics. At large, the concern rested in the fact that much of the faith in systems of intergovernmental governance such as UNESCO had been placed in the nation-state itself as the sole curator of chosen histories cultivated from the highest corridors of power (Smith 2006; Harrison 2013). In this process, marginal and undesired voices were often neglected, forgotten or oppressed. New ways of seeing and responding to these calls for identifying and supporting marginality soon emerged from within and beyond institutions. Institutional efforts to redress these imbalances included, for example, the 1979 Australia ICOMOS Guidelines for the Conservation of Places of Cultural Significance – the *Burra Charter*. This doctrinal document implicitly and explicitly recognised the entangled limits of heritage stewardship, illustrating how policies and governance had blindly presumed good faith of universalism and had heedlessly highjacked cosmopolitanism (Logan 2004; Waterton, Smith and Campbell 2006). In the US, a parallel effort to undo the alienation of minorities in the sphere of heritage resources resulted in the 1990 US Native American Graves Protection and Repatriation Act (Nash and Colwell 2020). In 1992, UNESCO established its World Heritage Center, an instrument of governance that supported participatory management planning and holistic conceptualisations of boundaries in the work of World Heritage designation (Jones, Bui and Ando 2022). UNESCO's apparent concern with a more inclusive form of governance eventually established doctrinal documents that support more diverse engagements with the idea of heritage, such as the 2003 Convention for the Safeguarding of the Intangible Cultural Heritage (Smith and Akagawa 2009). By 2015, the UN Sustainable Development goals included specific targets for heritage and preservation, later reimagined for the 2030 Agenda (Labadi et al. 2021). In sum, as the concept of heritage studies has expanded as a loose, yet clearly holistic, discipline, so too has the thick web of governance and diplomacy that simultaneously supports *and limits* its capacity.

The twenty-first century, marked by scholarly and institutional concerns with trauma, conflict, plunder and natural disasters, appeared to result in *more* policies, *more* assistance and *more* 'renowned' experts without a convincing rationale for the success and effectiveness of such a model of governance. During this time, the field of heritage studies had to grapple with the fact that rogue groups, many alienated by nation-states, had become adept masters of performativity by using the instruments and discourses of heritage safeguarding concerns for their own political and diplomatic transactions. These episodes took aim at spaces symbolically associated with their enemies: notable in 2001 at Bamiyan, Afghanistan; in 2012 in Timbuktu, Mali; and in 2015 at Palmyra, Syria (Gerstenblith 2005; Munawar 2017; Ba 2020). As heritage practitioners and institutions decried these attacks, many reflected on the legacies of violence embedded in global models of heritage governance. The shades of colonialism and neocolonial agendas still lurked behind promises of transparency and claims of collaboration.

At a local scale, concerns with governance take a different shape. Heritage is most often claimed as a 'public' good, and yet national budgets for heritage pale in comparison to military spending, for example. Ministries of culture are often tied (formally and informally) to the hope of tourism. Yet, structurally, this paradigm pivots on neoliberal agendas – hard currency returns on investment into the private sector, not direct return to *public* heritage spaces (Luke and Leeson 2022). As a result, conflicts of interest often perpetuate owing to failures of integration with urban planning, forestry, agriculture, water and extractive regimes (Baird 2013; Ahram 2015; Lane 2015; Samuels and Rico 2015; King 2019).

Many scholars in the early twenty-first century have broached this subject in sophisticated and detailed studies of heritage and diplomacy, making the study of governance at different scales a central theme in heritage studies and methodologies (see Kersel and Luke 2015 for an overview). Sophisticated historical approaches have revealed that the failure to realise collaborative governance does not necessarily lie in nation building as much as it does in disentangling the latent – yet pervasive – influence of imperialism. Deep historiography of the nineteenth century through the Cold War revealed that a history of cultural claims, such as the Athenian Parthenon, the Pergamon Altar or Copan casts, defined proximate power – nascent policies, laws and treaties aimed to regulate access to the past (Hamilakis 1999; Athanassopoulos 2002; Evans 2004; Gossman 2006). Western actors envisioned an international governing body after the collapse of empires, such as those that held sway at the 1919 Paris Peace Conference (Luke 2019). Some spaces for dialogue did result from the International Museum Office (IMO) and the

International Committee on Intellectual Cooperation (ICIC) under the League of Nations (Glendinning 2013), providing an institutional and, eventually, disciplinary, language to react to mass destruction and rebuilding at the end of World War II under the new regime of UNESCO. But there is an irony here: while multilateral conventions and guidelines are 'soft' measures theoretically intended to 'equalize the playing field' (allowing 'economically disadvantaged states to pursue policy standards in-country' and request international assistance for these), these are juxtaposed with 'hard' national laws protecting heritage from destruction, plunder and expropriation as a reaction to decades of such treatment by the same countries who might provide diplomatic aid (Kersel and Luke 2015, 77–8).

Ethnography has been the second ally to the project of revealing the diplomatic brokering and discursive manoeuvring that underpins decision-making in global heritage governance. Ethnographic approaches have the ability to tack between scales of analysis (the heritage site, the committee room), even as ever-expanding networks of communication and transport have blurred or redrawn the lines between the global and the local. Moreover, ethnographies of governance enable a perspective that examines how heritage value is produced through the social dynamics of both contexts (and everything in between) (Brumann and Berliner 2016). These methodologies have yielded more nuanced understandings of the persuasions affecting World Heritage inscription or, conversely, attributing 'at risk' status, and in particular the diplomatic weight of preservationist concerns relative to other priorities for multilateral support (Bertacchini et al. 2016; Brown et al. 2019; Liuzza and Meskell 2021). They have also provided a more thorough epistemic account of where scientific, and particularly anthropological, knowledge has set the terms of international heritage interventions. The result is that these become self-perpetuating, often to the detriment of constituencies looking to shift notions of heritage value towards something different and more relevant to their lives and livelihoods (Joy 2016). To a significant extent, the study of institutions and governance and the methodologies used to approach them have included a commitment to a critical study of ourselves – here

I refer to the primarily Western-driven educational systems of learning within and beyond the academy, institutional networks for heritage practitioners, and other tenets of both intellectual and social engineering that have solidified how we go about circulating and perpetuating heritage structures.

The limited success of international structures, the expense and bureaucracy of legal instruments and politics of policies call for a paradigm shift. Honest research into the grey areas that do not fit comfortably into *what is supposed to work* would be extremely helpful. If 'things' do not work as they *should*, then why does such governance continue? In order to disentangle the impression of policy progress, sustained analysis of the micropolitics that perpetuate these webs of power is required. Reports filled with text and graphics are just that, things with words and pictures. These 'decoys' distract public scrutiny precisely because the very institutions that produce them are supposed to be legitimate, global institutions. Major granting institutions continue to fund parachuting 'experts'/foreigners who too often fail to listen, to learn and to process specifics of a place, of a people – and the interconnectivity of their things. How, then, do we study governance and the structural situation(s) in which we currently find ourselves?

PRAXIS

Understanding the structures of governance requires work beyond accessing national and international legislation and identifying experts invested in heritage spaces. It requires a deep understanding of structural systems, of the governance apparatus itself (at the level of day-to-day bureaucratic working practices), and of funding, a process that, some would argue, needs to be learnt over a sustained period of experiential knowledge. Those heritage practitioners who have spent years doing fieldwork often gain an implicit perspective into this entangled web. Archaeologists, in particular, by gaining permission to peel back the layers of time, live the realities of informal and formal heritage governance. Confronting the power relationships that define access to dig, restore and study, these professionals see first-hand how binaries define what gets done (and what does not): rural versus urban, municipal versus private, foreign versus national. This complex web, and the fissures that it may reveal at all levels, becomes more impenetrable when studying decades-old global initiatives. At that end of the spectrum, outsiders assist with preparation of UNESCO dossiers, push international legislation to mitigate the trade in antiquities and offer guidance on military/terror preparedness for heritage protection. This generates an ecosystem that not only perpetuates impersonal approaches but also challenges what it means to act and think in local ways.

Here, ethnographic work is a vital component to holistic studies of heritage. Time spent 'in-country' requires a commitment to understanding how communities relate to each other. In knowing how structures operate, one may gauge opportunities, challenges and gross miscalculations. As an American who lives in Türkiye and works for a Turkish institution, I am eligible to apply for UK and EU grants as the local Turkish partner to work with colleagues based at institutions in Europe and the UK. Often these 'foreign' partners are Turkish, and we work from an established irony, both understanding the diplomatic rhetoric necessary to move forward. Yet, when reaching further afield to colleagues in the US, and American-granting institutions and foundations, just who is 'local' reflects an increasingly more textured and dynamic, and arguably more problematic, category. A 'local' person may be an in-country national citizen performing primarily a desk task for the ministry of culture, a person often engaged in top-down governance. We may also label those with greater proximity as local, such as a mayor or the leader in a local cooperative or civil society group. They may or may not hold college degrees and may or may not carry the experience and knowledge to really *know* a region (knowledge that now carries the label of intangible heritage). To study these complex roles requires years, not months, of deep engagement with customs and local historiographies. This can run counter to the Global North's obsession with 'reporting' from a week or so spent in the field, and to European and US-based university newsletters showcasing 'fieldwork opportunities'.

To the extent that ethnographic approaches involve actively working against rhetorical and structural pressures to distance governance and diplomacy from local conditions, this entails taking an especially critical approach to the language and *content* of participatory development: for instance, where 'community consultation' is in reality rubber-stamped, without due diligence or knowledge of the material conditions of these processes. For example, when working with practitioners exploring World Heritage status, archaeologists realised that despite decades of submitting detailed reports with maps, the experts from the respective ministry did not have access to this material – nor even known of its existence. The churning of bureaucracy had been so effective that everyone went dutifully about their respective duties: the archaeologist conducting the research, the regional authorities receiving four decades of annual reports and filing them (first tangibly, then digitally). Yet, no central system for baseline boundaries existed in a central location, resulting in fundamental flaws to new research and ignorance of how archaeologists had been negotiating (positively) with development sectors for decades. Those who utilise local archives know these types of scenes: three-ring binders with yellowing pages, often haphazardly piled on top of each other, or drawers of floppy disks, even CDs and now thumb drives that are no longer readable. In one case, I stared in dismay at a massive dark green (nearly black) 1960s cabinet locked with a fail-safe padlock. No one had a key. Someone said that a blow torch was the only thing possible to break the lock. We left it.

Solid research requires a strong foundation in disciplinary historiography alongside careful consideration of the historical sources used to understand changing governance over time. Archaeology in particular is a field wherein the production of knowledge (through excavation, survey, interpretation and communication) has been sustained and sponsored by national and international governance – as, for example, in US- and League of Nations-led efforts to promote archaeology in Türkiye during the early twentieth century, which formed the basis for more extensive collaboration in the service of regional economic development (Luke 2019). Archaeological data are thus the product of diplomatic relations, and vice versa. Linking these associations to shifts in strategies of governance requires precision in how one chooses to describe governance, and focusing on policy changes can provide both historical specificity and insight into networks of influence. Because policy can be more flexible and change more rapidly than law, tracing negotiation and transformation offers an opportunity to observe dialogue around key ideas (like heritage) and link these with 'punctuated periods' of revision that 'occur during the realignment of international territories, nation building, neoliberalism, and ... transnational corporatism' (Luke 2019, 11).

Language, too, matters when studying international phenomena through ethnography and history. Whether exploring Arabic or Ottoman Turkish records, French or German policies, we confront the rapidly disappearing commitment to language study. Artificial intelligence promises breakthroughs in translation services, yet arguably collaboration among scholars, each vested in their respective areas of expertise, results in holistic scholarship. This fluidity in boundaries also bridges cultural and educational fissures. While French or English are common benchmarks for programmes promising mutual understanding, this structure becomes a self-selecting revolving door of experts; in contrast, rarely do we find the same commitments to language from 'counter-part' or 'developing' nations. This structural violence for language learning is instilled in global social engineering of educational praxis, from organisations such as the International Baccalaureate Diploma with its limited range of support for *foundational levels* (non-native) in Arabic, Hebrew, Hindi, Indonesian, Japanese, Persian, Russian, Turkish, and so on, to BA, MA and even PhD programmes cutting language requirements. Are we fundamentally losing chances for a more engaged, global public and a critical aspect of heritage praxis? Has this practice implicitly instilled a path towards further sterilisation?

Our ability to analyse how we have arrived at this juncture is in part now obtainable in the digital revolution in archival research, but this is as much a research tool as it is yet another subject of cultural diplomacy – and, by extension, another way in which structural inequities can affect what research is actually conducted. The promise of digital humanities rests on objective and critical (re)learning of histories, both 'deep' prehistory and antiquity, and recent. International institutional archives have a major role to play in understanding foundational legacies. On the one hand we have the Japanese government's investment in digitising records of the League of Nations, making possible (for those fluent in English and French primarily) access to these. Investments by the World Bank and the International Monetary Fund, too, make possible a reading of these histories, again provided fluency in primarily English. The United Nations and for our purposes specifically UNESCO, too, has an increasingly vast digital repository, yet country-specific, heritage-related materials require advanced scheduling and in-person visits – limiting access to those facing financial boundaries as well as visa restrictions. Major national players have also laid bare their skeletons – such as the British National Archives (fee-based) and many presidential and other government-affiliated programmes, such as USAID, the JFK Library and the US Library of Congress. These help especially with imperial and Cold War historiographies.

Complementing these is the vast amount of information about where and how to find archival sources (in person and digitised) collections on the Middle East and North Africa through the Qatar Digital Library (including a translation interface) and Hazine. While national records may be available in-country, many ministries of culture and associated museums have yet to scan their histories. This is among the most challenging aspects of the digital turn. As the Global North has leveraged the opportunity to polish their tarnished pasts with a deluge of archival releases, and self-reflecting scholarship, many in the Global South now contend not only with capacity, but also a willingness to share their legacies. In this vein, we might look to the impressive work done by the British Museum, the Louvre, the Boston Museum of Fine Arts, the Metropolitan Museum of Art in New York, the National Museum of Antiquities in Leiden, the Hermitage in St. Petersburg, and the impressive and ongoing digitalisation of Ottoman Imperial Archives – open to in-person researchers in Istanbul. A vast array of newspapers and films (documentaries, news clips etc.), too, are available digitally.

TEACHING

Critical historiography of legal instruments, analysis of policy-led actions and conflict resolution can be taught through a combination of in-class sessions and real-world experience such as internships. Key to teaching about heritage governance is encouraging students to draw on their personal experiences of working across boundaries (linguistic, national, disciplinary) when these exist. Some of this intellectual and professional orientation can be encouraged in the setting of university training. For example, at Boston University (BU), I taught theoretical paradigms of heritage from the nineteenth century forward, complemented by an in-person visit to a space (park, exhibition, building) that explicitly and implicitly demonstrated what we were learning. For this course, I aggressively pursued the 30 per cent international student body of BU's incoming first-year classes who had attended International Baccalaureate Diploma programmes, and who implicitly understood what it meant to critically explore boundaries and were already bilingual, if not trilingual. Many had already visited (if not lived in) multiple different countries. This group was matched with American-based students interested in the 'the world', as they put it. This provided a foundation for engagement with global themes that complemented the underlying theoretical paradigms of landscape management and museums. Practically, this involved a World Heritage site or topic of the students' choice, where they explored rhetoric and syntax and questioned visual and audio choices. The variety of experiential backgrounds in this learning opportunity is invaluable. On this basis, students were ready to analyse new data within our model.

For this exercise, I drew from the US Ambassadors Fund for Cultural Preservation, which has been written about by few scholars – yet like World Heritage, there is sufficient data to dive into the nuances of boundaries and international platforms, as well as rhetoric and presentation. Among the results in 2008 was a Ukrainian student who argued that the US would do well to consider investing in eastern Ukraine and Crimea – she drew from not only the US reports, but also those of USAID and importantly

Ukrainian newspapers and civil society groups. In another example, a female student from Saudi Arabia problematised Olmstead's landscape paradigm from the perspective of Arabic (a language without a direct translation for the word *landscape*) and from the perspective of the Sky Bridge (300 metres) in Riyadh.

When I moved to Istanbul to teach at Koç University, I was required to teach in the CORE – an interdisciplinary sequence of classes meant to mirror the US liberal arts pedagogy. Adapting my US template to Istanbul has gone extremely well, yet also it has been different. For the graduate-level courses, I've scaled up the World Heritage component as literature has expanded, and as I come to understand student backgrounds, I scour new archives for case studies. Like the multilingual, international students at Boston University, I found this niche also in the Koç student body. I've learnt perspectives from Jordanian, Iranian, Russian, Pakistani, Italian, Serbian, Spanish and Turkish students that pale in comparison to the average US graduate-level seminar. For example, I've learnt about Crimea from the perspective of the Turkish Development Agency, the US Ambassadors Fund in Kosovo from a second-generation Balkan refugee film student, and US Department of State training programmes in Iraq and Afghanistan from a double International Relations – Archaeology and History of Art Turkish student (who also conducted fieldwork in Iraq).

The final projects done by students at Koç University rarely, if ever, invoke the 1931 Athens Charter or Osman Hamdi Bey's 1875 legislation set by the Imperial Museum in Constantinople, but in having learnt about the limits of these policies in the first part of my courses, students pivot fluidly in their analyses of contemporary issues. Instilling the understanding that technical assistance will not 'fix' plunder of heritage resources, nor will more legislation protect minority voices and heritage places, has been among my primary goals. What students learn is that heritage action and decision-making is drowning in the process and that heritage professionals and educators must work within thick bureaucracy created in the hopes of fostering mutual understanding. It is in the commitment to *be in place* that we *may* reach critical ways of thinking, analysing and working with people from different areas of the world. Thus, in making recommendations for teaching, I suggest focusing on modules in language training (the justification for it), cultural awareness protocols, historiography of national legal instruments and policies, historiography of international legal instruments and policies and rhetoric of diplomatic practice.

Classroom settings, however, can only accomplish so much. The UN Blue Line in southern Lebanon, for instance, cannot be studied from a desk. Heading south from the Tourist Landmark of the Resistance at Mleeta, my colleague and I learnt that Western-favoured passports will not get you through the rural interior checkpoint near Tayr Filsay, just beyond the Litani River crossing. This set of people must go the coastal route to reach the World Heritage site of Tyre. And, once at Tyre, for me, it was the experience *outside* the entrances that put this place into a *baseline* perspective: a Blue Shield sign riddled with bullet holes, UNIFIL jeeps carrying the logos of the many battalions deployed there, and the billboards with faces of martyrs provide a backdrop to the bustling market for fresh produce adjacent to the harbour. Call-outs to World Heritage were few, and even when present they are for the most part set behind fee-gates, often laced along the top with barbed wire. The crumbling modern 'dig house' – museum, research and administrative spaces – and crates and crates of decaying sherds from excavations took my breath away far more than the reconstructed stone monuments. As Shatha Abu-Khafajah (2019) pointed out during her presentation to my Koç students in Spring 2021: the early twentieth-century white suit worn by male archaeologists at least had the advantage of transparency: who controlled the money, permits, landscape and, thus, who underwrote what was presented as 'heritage'. As she argued, and my students agreed, today these relationships are often glossed under a rhetoric of collaboration that is far from transparent. Sustained field-based experience and ethnographic practice are baselines for how to unpack this rhetoric.

Where can one learn about the baseline aspects of studying and performing heritage diplomacy? I struggle to recommend specific readings precisely because each case does require a holistic and truthful look at legacies and futures in context. My fear is that we've become lost in the thicket of what we think will solve problems: policies, laws, circulars, mandates and updates. A method for learning heritage diplomacy, then, should begin at developing a way of thinking that recognises, and embraces, the essence of entanglement that stems from being in another's space and respecting one's position. Some proficiency in language, of course, goes a long way. Arrival with a translator positions one's presence differently – both formally but also intellectually. Your interlocutors will wonder how (if) you will be received by your hosts and how the ensuing partnership may develop. How can they be sure you will be an effective and positive force? In your movements, your clothing, your voice – your deference to cultural practice – you also implicitly communicate awareness and respect. Yet, you must also explicitly understand that your work will be challenging – and thus, you must also display a capacity for leadership. Hubris will not open doors, but cosmopolitanism with humility *may*. In closing, some of the primers that I hold to are:

- Make efforts to understand and slowly improve upon your abilities with language as well as cultural cues, even if fluency may be a very long-term goal; learn how to read a room for other cultural signals; dress appropriately; and focus on attainable outcomes.
- Know which settings are appropriate for which conversations and make time to visit and stay in-country if you are serious about capacity. Short, one-off trips, especially without sufficient preparation, will merely skim the surface, likely one polished for presentation, rather than tackle systemic challenges compassionately.

REFERENCES AND RESOURCES

Abu-Khafajah, Shatha and Riham Miqdadi. 2019. 'Prejudice, military intelligence, and neoliberalism: Examining the local within archaeology and heritage practices in Jordan'. *Contemporary Levant* 4(2): 92–106.

Ahram, Ariel I. 2015. 'Development, counterinsurgency, and the destruction of the Iraqi marshes'. *International Journal of Middle East Studies* 47(3): 447–66.

Athanassopoulos, Effie-Fotini. 2002. 'An "ancient" landscape: European ideals, archaeology, and nation building in early modern Greece'. *Journal of Modern Greek Studies* 20(2): 273–305.

Ba, Oumar. 2020. 'Contested meanings: Timbuktu and the prosecution of destruction of cultural heritage as war crimes'. *African Studies Review* 63(4): 743–62.

Baird, Melissa F. 2013. '"The breath of the mountain is my heart": Indigenous cultural landscapes and the politics of heritage'. *International Journal of Heritage Studies* 19(4): 327–40.

Bertacchini, Enrico, Claudia Liuzza, Lynn Meskell and Donatella Saccone. 2016. 'The politicization of UNESCO World Heritage decision making'. *Public Choice* 167: 95–129.

Brown, Nicholas E., Claudia Liuzza, and Lynn Meskell. 2019. 'The politics of peril: UNESCO's List of World Heritage in Danger'. *Journal of Field Archaeology* 44(5): 287–303.

Betts, Paul. 2015. 'The warden of World Heritage: UNESCO and the rescue of the Nubian Monuments'. *Past & Present* 226(suppl_10): 100–125.

Betts, Paul and Corey Ross. 2015. 'Modern historical preservation: Towards a global perspective'. *Past & Present* 226 (suppl. 10): 7–26.

Brumann, Christoph and David Berliner. 2016. 'Introduction: UNESCO world heritage – grounded?' In *World Heritage on the Ground: Ethnographic perspectives*, edited by Christoph Brumann and David Berliner, 1–34. Oxford: Berghahn.

Cleere, Henry. 2011. 'The 1972 UNESCO World Heritage Convention'. *Heritage & Society* 4(2): 173–86.

Dromgoole, Sarah. 2013. *Underwater Cultural Heritage and International Law*. Vol. 101. Cambridge: Cambridge University Press.

Evans, R Tripp. 2004. *Romancing the Maya: Mexican antiquity in the American imagination, 1820–1915*. Austin, TX: University of Texas Press.

Gerstenblith, Patty. 2005. 'From Bamiyan to Baghdad: Warfare and the preservation of cultural heritage at the beginning of the 21st century'. *Georgetown Journal of International Law* 37: 245.

Gerstenblith, Patty. 2008. *Art, Cultural Heritage, and the Law: Cases and materials*. 2nd ed. Durham. NC: Carolina Academic Press.

Gerstenblith, Patty. 2014. 'Beyond the 1954 Hague Convention'. In *Cultural Awareness in the Military: Developments and implications for future humanitarian cooperation*, edited by Robert Albro and Bill Ivey, 83–98. New York: Palgrave Macmillan.

Glendinning, Miles. 2013. *The Conservation Movement: A history of architectural preservation: Antiquity to modernity*. New York: Routledge.

Gossman, Lionel. 2006. 'Imperial icon: The Pergamon Altar in Wilhelminian Germany'. *The Journal of Modern History* 78(3): 551–87.

Hamilakis, Yannis. 1999. 'Stories from exile: Fragments from the cultural biography of the Parthenon (or "Elgin") marbles'. *World Archaeology: The Cultural Biography of Objects* 31(2): 303–20.

Harrison, Rodney. 2013. *Heritage: Critical approaches*. New York: Routledge.

Jones, Thomas E., Huong T. Bui and Katsuhiro Ando. 2022. 'Zoning for world heritage sites: Dual dilemmas in development and demographics'. *Tourism Geographies* 24(1): 33–55.

Joy, Charlotte L. 2016. *The Politics of Heritage Management in Mali: From UNESCO to Djenné*. New York: Routledge.

Kersel, Morag M. 2015. 'Storage wars: Solving the archaeological curation crisis?' *Journal of Eastern Mediterranean Archaeology & Heritage Studies* 3(1): 42–54.

King, Rachel. 2019. *Outlaws, Anxiety, and Disorder in Southern Africa: Material histories of the Maloti-Drakensberg*. Cham: Springer.

Labadi, Sophia, Francesca Giliberto, Ilaria Rosetti, Linda Shetabi and Ege Yildirim. 2021. *Heritage and the Sustainable Development Goals: Policy guidance for heritage and development actors*. ICOMOS report.

Lane, Paul. 2015. *Primordial Conservationists, Environmental Sustainability, and the Rhetoric of Pastoralist Cultural*

Heritage in East Africa. Boulder, CO: University Press of Colorado.

Liuzza, Claudia and Lynn Meskell. 2021. 'Power, persuasion and preservation: Exacting times in the World Heritage Committee'. *Territory, Politics, Governance* 11(7): 1265–80.

Logan, William. 2004. 'Voices from the periphery: The Burra Charter in context'. *Historic Environment* 18(1): 2–8.

Luke, Christina. 2019. *A Pearl in Peril: Heritage and diplomacy in Turkey*. New York: Oxford University Press.

Luke, Christina and Morag M. Kersel. 2013. *US Cultural Diplomacy and Archaeology: Soft power, hard heritage*. London: Routledge.

Luke, Christina and Madison M. Leeson. 2022. 'UNESCO-UNDP tourism and security in Cold War Turkey and Iran'. *Journal of Heritage Tourism* 17(6): 669–84.

Meskell, Lynn. 2018. *A Future in Ruins: UNESCO, World Heritage, and the dream of peace*. New York: Oxford University Press.

Munawar, Nour A. 2017. 'Reconstructing cultural heritage in conflict zones: Should Palmyra be rebuilt?' *Ex Novo: Journal of Archaeology* 2: 33–48.

Nash, Stephen E. and Chip Colwell. 2020. 'NAGPRA at 30: The effects of repatriation'. *Annual Review of Anthropology* 49: 225–39.

Samuels, Kathryn Lafrenz and Trinidad Rico. 2015. *Heritage Keywords: Rhetoric and redescription in cultural heritage*. Boulder, CO: University Press of Colorado.

Smith, Laurajane. 2006. *Uses of Heritage*. London: Routledge.

Smith, Laurajane and Natsuko Akagawa (eds) 2009. *Intangible Heritage*. London: Routledge.

Waterton, Emma, Laurajane Smith and Gary Campbell. 2006. 'The utility of discourse analysis to heritage studies: The Burra Charter and social inclusion', *International Journal of Heritage Studies* 12(4): 339–55.

10 On locality

Yujie Zhu

In the field of heritage studies, scholars often focus on the influence of heritage discourse on locality and the local, which encompasses a range of interconnected issues. These issues include the impact of heritage on local communities, the significance of territory and landscape and the shaping of senses of place. Locality serves as a dynamic setting in which heritage practices take place and is shaped by the policies of international and national agencies as well as local governance, institutions and policies.

Locality has traditionally been perceived as a confined and secure space associated with custodianship and stewardship. However, our contemporary world necessitates a critical re-examination of this understanding. It is imperative to acknowledge that locality is intricately connected to scales beyond immediate or physical boundaries, including the national and international, through the flow of information, people, policies and exchanges. Furthermore, it is crucial to acknowledge the performative nature of the local. The concept of locality is not a fixed or objective reality; rather, it is a social construct that is actively shaped and utilised by various stakeholders within the heritage field (Zhu 2018).

Therefore, conducting research on heritage is essential for critically examining the concept of locality and revealing the inherent power dynamics and politics it encompasses, particularly with regard to exclusion and inclusion. When examined through the lens of ethnography, various questions arise: Who has the authority to define locality? Which actors possess the power to represent local values and interests? Who has been included and excluded in these power dynamics? Is local belonging an outcome of expert-driven constructions, a consequence of grassroots knowledge production or a collaborative effort among various stakeholders?

In addressing these questions, I employ an approach that focuses on the interface between heritage and tourism to critically examine the notion of locality. Within the realm of international organisations like UNESCO, there is often a perception that tourism poses a threat to the authenticity of localities. Consequently, efforts have been made to safeguard and preserve the integrity of these places. However, this viewpoint perpetuates a colonial perspective that treats locality as a spectacle or zoo-like attraction.

To enhance our understanding, it is crucial to transcend the simplistic paradigm of threat and preservation, as well as the dichotomy between external–local or host and guest. Such paradigms often run the risk of marginalising the perspectives of other relevant actors. Rather, locality could be acknowledged as a dynamic contact zone that involves a multitude of values and interests, from all involved parties, through processes of negotiation and contestation.

In my previous research on heritage tourism in Lijiang, China, I conducted long-term ethnography that allowed me to observe how tourists engage with heritage. Rather than viewing them solely as external visitors, I discovered that many tourists have become integrated into local communities and establish a unique experience that lies somewhere between tourism and migration (Zhu 2012). These individuals bring their own knowledge and values from external sources, yet they also incorporate local culture into their everyday lives. The performative nature of everyday life blurs the boundaries between tourists and locals, as the tourists themselves become locals through their interactions and engagement. Moreover, the locals involved in the tourism business have performed the role of cultural brokers, mediating between heritage and external capital. As a result, the heritage site of Lijiang has become a contact zone where different communities come together to perform and exchange their heritage practices, stories and interests. The distinction between so-called locals and tourists becomes less clear in this context.

In this process of interaction between heritage and tourism, locality, as a social construct, is not fixed but is performed and enacted through the actions, discourses and representations of these actors involved in heritage practices. They strategically deploy the concept of locality to advance their own interests, seek recognition and assert their cultural identities. Their understanding and representation of locality can become fluid as a result of the negotiation and communication inherent in presenting their locality and authenticity to the external world.

This approach of examining the interface between heritage and tourism helps transcend the notion of locality as a simplistic, secure and static zone. Instead, it reveals that the impact of tourism extends beyond local boundaries, influencing heritage practices, commodification and cultural exchange. The heritage tourism space allows for the exchange of ideas, interaction and collaboration beyond physical boundaries, enabling the formation of trans-local networks and connections.

The broader implications of this intervention invite critical reflection on research methods in heritage studies. This discussion aims to move beyond research methods confined to particular scales and instead situates itself within the broader methodological framework of the politics of scale within heritage studies (Lähdesmäki, Thomas and Zhu 2019). Heritage is not confined to a single scale, whether it be local, national, regional or international. Instead, heritage operates and transforms across multiple scales as processes of localisation and relocalisation. Rather than perceiving locality as a static zone, such an approach can move away from simplistic understandings of a power dynamic solely between a central authority (representing international and national entities) and the periphery (representing locality), and instead recognises the existence of multiple centres engaged in a continuous dialogue without excluding voices from actors, such as the tourists. By embracing the politics of scale in heritage studies, and situating locality within this framework, we develop a more comprehensive understanding of heritage dynamics in our contemporary world.

REFERENCES AND RESOURCES

Lähdesmäki, Tuuli, Suzie Thomas and Yujie Zhu (eds) 2019. *Politics of Scale: New directions in critical heritage studies*. Vol. 1. New York: Berghahn Books.

Zhu, Yujie. 2012. 'Performing heritage: Rethinking authenticity in tourism'. *Annals of Tourism Research* 39(3): 1495–1513.

Zhu, Yujie. 2018. *Heritage and Romantic Consumption in China*. Amsterdam: Amsterdam University Press.

11 Landscapes and environment

Melissa F. Baird

DESCRIPTION AND HISTORIOGRAPHY

This contribution examines landscapes *as* heritage. Heritage landscapes, as defined here, include 'urban, Indigenous, and post-industrial landscapes, wildlife management and wilderness areas, archaeological sites, coastal and marine environments, community-conserved areas, [and] land-trust preserves' (Baird 2017, 5). Heritage landscapes are places where histories, memories and cultures converge. Although they are often viewed as places on a map – for example, an archaeological site or a historic urban landscape – they are also central to how a community negotiates and makes meaning. Here, I focus primarily on the socio-political contexts of heritage landscapes: the political dynamics and cultural connections, the 'frictions' and how these sites are often sites of power and control (after Tsing 2005). As a global industry, heritage engages experts who negotiate and define policy issues that have far-reaching impacts for communities of connection (Rico 2008).

From a conceptual perspective, heritage landscapes are both material, encompassing physical and ecological features, and intangible, comprising histories, meaning and memories (Bender 2020). Landscapes are commonly separated into two categories: natural and cultural. Natural landscapes include geographical areas primarily shaped by natural processes, such as landforms or volcanoes. In contrast, cultural landscapes are connected to and transformed through human activities and include community land use practices and rituals. Landscapes are dynamic, relational, contested and contingent. Yet, many earlier studies kept a narrow focus on the materiality or aesthetics of a landscape. In academic and professional settings, understanding the complexity of landscapes provides insights into both the lived connections and political changes that lead to conflicts (for example, Cosgrove and Daniels 1988; Ingold 1993; Bird Rose 1996; Taçon 1999; Byrne 2003; Carruthers 2003; Hardesty 2003; Layton and Ucko 1999; Blue Spruce and Thrasher 2009; Fontein 2006; Prosper 2007; Taylor and Lennon 2011).

The study of heritage landscapes – its early approaches, methods, sources and theoretical frameworks – can be traced to the Enlightenment intellectual movement. The project of cultural thinking during the eighteenth century emphasised reason, scientific enquiry, progress and faith in systems governed by laws. This conception viewed humans as separate from the 'natural world' and 'Nature'. At the same time, imperialist ambitions and territorial expansions engendered a rush to accumulate and catalogue not only landscapes but also the resources within. Explorers – cartographers, missionaries, prospectors and scientists – mapped and renamed places and peoples. These acts constitute a form of erasure and production, and these early constructions worked to frame how we understand people attach meanings to place (for example, Heidegger 1977; Ingold 1993; Taylor and Lennon 2011). The emergence of National Parks, for example, and their value as wilderness was simply a projection of earlier visions of Nature as sublime, inanimate and devoid of people. They are also ideological constructions of identity that found great resonance and were transported across the globe and are still reflected in modern legal policies and management practices today.

In the mid-twentieth century, archaeologists explored the meaning of material remains of individual sites and their broader social and spatial contexts; they reconstructed past uses of landscapes to understand societal changes. The processual archaeologists of the 1960s and 1970s drew criticism for an over-reliance on positivist methods that focused on the environment without consideration of local, situated contexts. A perennial issue, however, was how culture is produced and expressed spatially or how landscapes denote articulations between people and place. In recent decades, social scientists and communities have played a pivotal role in reframing understandings of heritage landscapes beyond their physical settings, for example, how landscapes are reconfigured for capitalist expansions (Harvey and Perry 2015) or within political projects. Scholars today are moving away from top-down understandings to more historically nuanced studies, adopting multidisciplinary and multivocal approaches that understand landscapes as socially and culturally constituted (see McGuire 1991). The motivation is to think past the value within a landscape to forge new understandings centred on revisioning and remapping that are relational and focused on community-led and driven understandings.

Still, the connection between how we understand landscapes and how we manage landscapes is often not apparent. The policy *of* landscapes is often where we see the most tensions. For example, the United Nations Educational, Scientific and Cultural Organization (UNESCO) World Heritage Committee's 1992 cultural landscapes' designation was intended to correct the overrepresentation of Western European and natural heritage properties and the underrepresentation of Indigenous people's heritage. Yet, as argued elsewhere, this approach frustrated efforts by silencing the communities connected to the sites through positioning heritage managers as experts. It is a thorny issue, as experts are also constrained by their disciplinary foci and within the organisation's mission. Nevertheless, UNESCO and other organisations are working to respond to these criticisms and have created policies and approaches to address the inflexibility of the bureaucratic apparatus and the role of nation-states in mediating claims. Today, the goal is to lean towards inclusivity and prioritise descendant communities in interpreting, protecting and understanding heritage sites.

When thinking about the politics of knowledge-making, heritage landscapes are excellent for bringing in diverse approaches, especially around their 'value'. Value is directly observable; it can be traced through actions – such as how a site is interpreted, preserved and recognised. For example, the value of post-industrial landscapes can be found by investigating how they are used to promote tourism development. That is, how communities leverage the history of extraction to generate revenue (Sørhaug 2021). However, assigning value can have consequences for stakeholders.

For example, the Cypress Hills region in southeastern Alberta holds historical value and significance for Indigenous communities and European settlers' descendants. Conflicts often relate to value – but are often framed as conflicts over site management (Robertson 2002; Oetelaar and Oetelaar 2006; Amundsen-Meyer 2015). The real issue of determining value is in recognition that some stakeholders see their concerns related to misrepresentation or appropriation, or worse, dispossession and cultural erasures.

My early interest in heritage landscapes emerged through my training as an archaeologist. When I shifted to a project on the landscapes in the Mongolian Altai, I drew insights from the seminal writings of social theorists of practice theory and phenomenology and postcolonial critiques (see e.g. Bourdieu 1977; Casey 1996; Tilley 1994). Of interest were how various scholars have articulated with landscapes to raise new questions about socio-political contexts, as well as themes such as dwelling (Basso 1996; Heidegger 1977) borders (Barkan and Shelton 1998), diaspora, globalisation (Tsing 2003) and race (Moore, Pandian and Kosek 2003; Coumans 2011). Yet, these studies did not necessarily provide a way to understand the history of meaning-making and its relation to the glossing, omissions and retelling of heritage landscapes. How are these places also sites of political struggles and mediated by powerful global-relations agents (Baird 2009, 2017; Harrison 2012; Lane 2015; see also Smith 2006)?

One way in is to engage with scholars who are expounding on issues of heritage, or revisiting or leveraging new approaches to understand debates. For example, studies in critical heritage and assemblage theory provide new directions and focal points. Assemblage theory has provided a generative space to redirect towards the connections, interactions and meanings shaped by context and associations. For example, this approach provides a view into how landscapes are constructed through historical processes and mediated within political struggles and knowledge claims. Or how heritage landscapes are recognised as sites of memory, belonging and cultural negotiation, and sites of conflict, displacement and loss (Baird 2017). Assemblage theory foregrounds diverse experiences and complex histories, but also provides a way to account for how expertise is deployed to promote political interests (Hamilakis and Meirion Jones 2017). This centring of political machinations provides unique insights into how identities are legitimised or how institutions shape heritage landscapes to suit their agendas or occlude complex relationships and legacies (Weiss 2014). At the same time, the potential disciplinary incompatibilities between how heritage landscapes are theorised and how communities imagine them must be addressed. How are heritage landscapes reconfiguring or engendering contradictory understandings? And how best to envision histories that prioritise and bring in multivocality and position historically excluded voices as the centre?

PRAXIS

What lies at the intersection of theory and practice and the deliberate framing of heritage landscapes *as* resources? In this conception, resources include multiple touch points: cultural and historical value, archaeological significance, tourism and economic benefits and educational opportunities. Resources could be material (for example, waste) or applied (for example, tourism). This conception also provides a way to deploy the concept of the extractive zone – the places where heritage, ecologies and communities converge. Extractive zones are central to the business of heritage landscapes.

A resource-attentive praxis seeks to change theoretical categories and practices by creating probing questions that show heritage landscapes as multifaceted, transactional and interdependent. Specifically, what are the analytic categories, and are they responsive to new directions and interpretations? Is there merit in considering heritage landscapes and resource areas together, and what are the interpretive possibilities for understanding how power and knowledge are embedded in relations (Foucault 1979)? Foregrounding heritage landscapes as sites of power helps reveal how they merge and clash with economic value, energy production, industry, infrastructure development and environmental issues.

I draw here from a multi-year and multisited project that applied archaeological, ethnographic and 'forensic' methods to understand heritage in extractive zones. My most recent project, for example, was a three-year investigation of Oregon's now cancelled but highly contested energy development projects: the Jordan Cove Energy Project and the Pacific Connector Pipeline. The region encompasses diverse stakeholders and an extensive heritage landscape inventory, including traditional cultural properties, fishing and resource industries, marine reserves and robust tourism industries. Methodologically, the project integrated ethnographic, historical and archival and landscape archaeology approaches. I aimed to understand how heritage work was enacted in extractive contexts, especially how varied stakeholders and local communities made sense of an in-progress development rush. Questions centred on how communities organised their strategies and whether they invoked heritage to validate claims, gain access or create meaning. As I found, heritage landscapes played a central role in legitimising claims. Whether it was communities occupying protest camps or scientists mobilising the policy process, heritage landscapes were central to and taken up to gain legitimacy and access. Locating heritage landscapes within extractive contexts brings into sharper focus their centrality in encounters among communities, industries and the state.

Praxis goes beyond measuring and mapping. It involves complex engagements, entanglements and concerns about how we *do* heritage landscape research. The praxis of heritage landscapes then involves all stages – from how you approach your research, the places you choose to work, and the political commitments and awareness you bring to your work (Pollock 2008). By paying attention to heritage landscapes as resources, scholars can gain insights into socio-ecological relations and different conceptual, material, economic and cultural contexts. I chose this approach to constrain and expand: focusing on 'resources' opens up methodologies to a wide range of interconnected and reinforcing constraints. Not only to get a clearer picture of heritage landscapes as a resource, but also to trace the inextricable connection to extracted resources (see DeSilvey 2017).

Yet, investigating such places can be challenging due to their dynamic nature and global reach. There are often implicit challenges in investigating places beyond the ethnographic. These fast-moving places require a different approach – one that can tack between the local and global (Crate and Nuttall 2009; Harvey 2015; DeSilvey 2017). The most appealing methods to me are activist oriented and integrate approaches to understand place-based global interactions. Eyal Weizman's (2012) work, particularly his forensic architecture method, is valuable for understanding heritage landscapes in the extractive zones. This forensic approach challenges constructed truths and narratives to expose mechanisms and systems of power. Take, for example, the outpost – which is a heritage landscape in the West Bank. Weizman's team illustrates how the outpost functions as a stake: once established, the area is cordoned off, restricting access and claims. This cordon creates a third space, complete with a new set of regulations and rules of engagement. These rules dictate, for example, who is allowed entry, how evidence is preserved, how procedures are carried out and who has jurisdiction. Once these are established, evidence is categorised, facts are surmised, maps are drawn, boundaries are policed and insiders and outsiders are identified.

Adopting a forensic praxis to understand a heritage landscape that is also a proposed industrial development site, one could investigate and trace the specific ways that industries mobilise heritage. For example, do companies introduce new rules and regulations? Are heritage landscapes being redefined into industry assets? Is the site's industrial past used to promote new understandings? A forensic praxis provides a way to investigate claims and check facts and 'submitted' evidence, and is essential to tracing and making sense of social conflicts that often arise in extraction sites (for example, Howitt 1992; Sawyer 2004; Luning 2012; Breglia 2013; Kirsch 2014; Storm 2014; Coombe and Baird 2016). As these studies and my work have found, conflicts are intricately linked with environmental vulnerability, Indigenous heritage, heritage policy and corporate place-making in industrial zones. Yet, at the same time, extractive zones are fast paced and often hard to follow. An action and activist praxis considers multiple and dynamic processes at play to reveal, for example, the hidden costs often borne by frontline communities, both human and more than human. What does this look like? Ethnographic engagements at protest sites, counter-mapping industry reports of cultural resources as a form of shareholder activism or analysing public comments in policy – such as the National Environmental Policy Act (NEPA) and known archaeological data. For example, my analyses of industry archaeological reports in Pacific NorthWest LNG in British Columbia found inconsistencies and a lack of citations to archaeological reports of the region. Specifically, the reports failed to mention the extensive heritage inventory and history of site investigations nearby in Prince Rupert as a 'flagship region in Northwest Coast prehistory' (see Ames and Martindale 2014, 140).

Integrating multiple methods and combining on-the-ground landscape studies alongside ethnography, archival research methods and discourse analysis enables scholars to anchor encounters. That is, it involves bringing together seemingly disparate data sources (for example, archives, investor reports, landscape and GIS data) in an investigative approach to examine how industry and the state work through heritage. The goal is to provide a throughline to explore the transformations of heritage landscapes and to trace how transnational actors and local communities negotiate access to resources: raw materials, labour or industry-friendly policies.

In post-industrial contexts, a focus on heritage materiality – especially waste – holds great promise (Gordillo 2014; Armerio 2021; Liboiron 2021; Baird 2022). As Gordillo (2014, 11) posited, reckoning with the 'on-the-ground traces of places that have been destroyed' allows us insights into the nature of these engagements. These traces, or waste, are more than a 'thing' – something discarded; they provide evidence and are connected through social, political and economic spheres (Baird 2022). Like place-making, waste-making is layered with meaning (after Basso 1996, 7). Waste mediates how people interact with the world. Yet, although ubiquitous, waste is often ignored. Focusing on waste as a resource in extractive heritage landscapes provides a forward-thinking praxis that could integrate approaches, such as participatory mapping, photovoice or storywork methods. A shift towards more inclusive and decolonised approaches could involve transferring management responsibilities to local communities, integrating traditional knowledge and science, and coordinating efforts across national boundaries. With a global rush to extract resources and the projected loss from climate impacts ongoing, raising questions of how to render these engagements ethnographically visible is essential.

TEACHING

Teaching approaches to heritage landscapes necessitates viewing from substantive and action-oriented perspectives to grasp their significance and implications. How can pedagogy and practice support student and practitioner understandings of heritage landscapes that transcend limitations and establish productive engagements? It can do so through a process of engaged pedagogy that fosters critical thinking, investigating heritage landscapes beyond places on a map. By way of example, to study the United States/Mexico border – as a heritage landscape, a metaphor, a boundary – would require the tools to understand how a border marks space and the people within it are marked in racial, ethnic and social terms. Understanding these boundaries and conflict 'landscapes' could involve examining how race, class, gender and nationality impact lived experience. It would also require a historical and methodological approach to furnish a keen sense of what came before, how scholars engaged with these concepts and how current research and its connections are deployed.

Training students in these approaches could provide a comprehensive perspective that encompasses both the pragmatic implications of landscapes as heritage, especially in managing them, and their ethical use. Although students may complain that the study of cultural heritage management can be dry, it is where the work of heritage is most often deployed. Examples include understanding how a site's protected status can change depending on political whims (Bears Ears National Monument) or be impacted by climate change (for example, the Great Barrier

Reef in Australia) or war-induced migration and abandonment (the Syrian Civil War). Students would be encouraged to investigate and differentiate how scholars and practitioners engage with, think about and apply heritage policies. That is, they would be encouraged to think through how epistemological and ontological orientations have constituted the landscape and how these intersect with and relate to contemporary heritage policies and practices. Part and parcel of this task would be to unpack and understand terms such as place (as socially constructed) and space (as physical settings). How are these distinct but also connected? What are the various knowledge claims and epistemological underpinnings?

To develop multidimensional understandings, bring in multiple perspectives and connect these understandings to contemporary negotiations, teaching modules could combine methods and approaches. For example, one could undertake a case study analysis or combine ethnographic, participatory mapping and geographic information systems (GIS) with archival analyses. Participatory mapping, for example, would provide a method to collect and integrate community knowledge and perceptions of the landscape. Combined with GIS, these data could be analysed spatially using topographic maps and demographic or census data to understand relationships. This methodological training could also include applying archival analyses of historical maps and documents or photographs that could provide more detailed historical context. Whatever the combination, the goal is to broaden perspectives of heritage landscapes.

One compelling approach would be to train students to think about heritage landscapes within a political and activist frame. From mass protests to grassroots campaigns, extractive heritage sites often function as training grounds or spaces for groups to direct action and elevate their concerns. Whether it is First Nation groups protesting a proposed development project through their territories or industries showcasing a region's mining history to garner public support, each draw on heritage to make claims (see Baird 2017). Students need to learn skills that can follow the action. For example, one approach is participatory research that follows the on-the-ground conflicts related to protecting a sacred site. Students learn how to design a project that combines fieldwork, archival research, GIS or digital mapping. In the field, students could undertake direct observation and participate by interviewing activists or observing demonstrations. Or they could engage in a collaborative partnership with activists or local organisations, helping with initiatives while also gaining experience in the policy process. Or, alternatively, students could work in the archives, locating and analysing government reports and documents, newspaper archives, historical maps or diaries. Combined with discourse analysis of contemporary framings, using social media, public comments or newspaper articles, students could understand how industry and communities are each framing the issues or using public opinion, the courts or the policy process to assert rights and make claims.

A forensic approach presents a unique opportunity to bring in various disciplinary backgrounds in innovative ways. For example, I drew on my past training as an archaeologist to ground-truth reports and counter-map proposed sites. I used company reports, historical surveys and an informal landscape survey to see if these data contrasted with the official maps and reports. I also used other strategies to refine my understanding. I submitted a Freedom of Information (FOIA) request (unsuccessful) and purchased a single share in a Canadian energy company to gain access to annual reports and stakeholder meetings. Learning how to follow the complicated permitting process, reports, community events and regulatory agencies is essential to understanding heritage landscapes today.

One approach is to provide students with a way to bring in a student's position and expertise as a valid entry point. An example of this approach would be an engineering student in fluid dynamics working with a social scientist or historian to map and model pollutants and their connection to heritage places. In this way, the students could connect seemingly disparate data to understand the implications of existing policies and laws, permitting processes and impacts on communities of connections who often bear the disproportionate burden of industrial pollution. The goal is always to think of new ways to capture and apply data sets that may be overlooked, such as using GIS alongside documentary records to understand climatic and social data. Combining documentary data (newspapers, diaries, interviews) and combining these with present-day industry reports opens up the kinds of sources we can use and new ways to approach projects. Whatever the case, creativity, including multiple voices, and attention to alternative modes of thinking would be highly encouraged. The intention is to bring in their experiences and insights for stakeholders beyond the academy. And to challenge assumptions and to understand heritage landscapes as sites that are often sites of contradictory and contested visions.

REFERENCES AND RESOURCES

Ames, Kenneth M. and Andrew Martindale. 2014. 'Rope bridges and cables: A synthesis of Prince Rupert Harbour archaeology'. *Canadian Journal of Archaeology/Journal Canadien d'Archéologie* 38(1): 140–78.

Amundsen-Meyer, Lindsay. 2015. 'Creating a spatial dialogue: A'kee Piskun and attachment to place on the Northwestern Plains'. *Plains Anthropologist* 60(234): 124–49.

Apaydin, Veysel. 2020. *Critical Perspectives on Cultural Memory and Heritage: Construction, transformation, and destruction*. London: UCL Press.

Armerio, Marco. 2021. *Wasteocene: Stories from the global dump*. Cambridge: Cambridge University Press.

Baird, Melissa F. 2009. 'The politics of place: Heritage, identity, and the epistemologies of cultural landscapes'. PhD thesis, University of Oregon.

Baird, Melissa F. 2017. *Critical Theory and the Anthropology of Heritage Landscapes*. Gainesville, FL: University Press of Florida.

Baird, Melissa F. 2022. 'Waste sits in places: Post-extractive landscapes as heritage'. In *Landscape as Heritage*, edited by Giacomo Pettenati, 204–15. London: Routledge.

Barkan, Elazar and Marie-Denise Shelton. 1998. *Borders, Exiles, Diasporas*. Stanford, CA: Stanford University Press.

Basso, Keith H. 1996. *Wisdom Sits in Places: Landscapes and language among the Western Apache*. Albuquerque, NM: University of New Mexico Press.

Bender, Barbara. 2020. 'Landscape and politics'. In *The Material Culture Reader*, edited by Victor Buchli, 135–74. New York: Routledge.

Bird Rose, Deborah. 1996. *Nourishing Terrains: Australian Aboriginal views of landscape and wilderness*. Canberra: Australian Heritage Commission.

Blue Spruce, Duane Blue and Tanya Thrasher. 2009. *The Land Has Memory: Indigenous knowledge, native landscapes, and the National Museum of the American Indian*. Chapel Hill, NC: University of North Carolina Press.

Bourdieu, Pierre. 1977. *Outline of a Theory of Practice*. Cambridge: Cambridge University Press.

Breglia, Lisa. 2013. *Living with Oil: Promises, peaks, and declines on Mexico's Gulf coast*. Austin, TX: University of Texas Press.

Byrne, Denis. 2003. 'Nervous landscapes: Race and space in Australia'. *Journal of Social Archaeology* 32: 169–93.

Carruthers, Jane. 2003. 'Contesting cultural landscapes in South Africa and Australia: Comparing the significance of the Kalahari Gemsbok and Uluru-Kata Tjuta national parks'. In *Disputed Territories: Land, culture, and identity in settler societies*, edited by David Trigger and Gareth Griffiths, 233–68. Hong Kong: Hong Kong University Press.

Casey, Edward S. 1996. 'How to get from space to place in a fairly short stretch of time: Phenomenological prolegomena'. In *Senses of Place*, edited by Steven Feld and Keith H. Basso, 3–12. Santa Fe, NM: School of American Research Press.

Coombe, Rosemary J. and Melissa Baird. 2016. 'The limits of heritage: Corporate interests and cultural rights on resource frontiers'. In A *Companion to Heritage Studies*, edited by William Logan, Máiréad Nic Craith and Ullrich Kockel, 337–54. Chichester: Wiley & Sons Publishing.

Cosgrove, Denis and Stephen Daniels. 1988. *The Iconography of Landscape: Essays on the symbolic representation, design, and use of past environments*. Cambridge: Cambridge University Press.

Coumans, Catherine. 2011. 'Occupying spaces created by conflict: Anthropologists, development NGOs, responsible investment, and mining'. *Current Anthropology* 52(S3): 29–43.

Crate, Susan and Mark Nuttall (eds) 2009. *Anthropology and Climate Change: From encounters to action*. Walnut Creek, CA: Left Coast Press.

DeSilvey, Caitlin. 2017. *Curated Decay: Heritage beyond saving*. Minneapolis, MN: University of Minnesota Press.

Fontein, Joost. 2006. *The Silence of Great Zimbabwe: Contested landscapes and the power of heritage*. London: UCL Press.

Foucault, Michel. 1979. *Discipline and Punish: The birth of the prison*. London: Vintage Books.

Gokee, Cameron and Jason de León. 2014. 'Sites of contention'. *Journal of Contemporary Archaeology* 1(1): 133–63.

Gordillo, Gastón R. 2014. *Rubble: The afterlife of destruction*. Durham, NC: Duke University Press.

Hamilakis, Yannis and Andrew Meirion Jones. 2017. 'Archaeology and assemblage'. *Cambridge Archaeological Journal* 27(1): 77–84.

Hardesty, Donald. 2003. 'Mining rushes and landscape learning in the modern world'. In *Colonization of Unfamiliar Landscapes: The archaeology of adaptation*, edited by Marcy Rockman and James Steele, 81–96. London: Routledge.

Harrison, Rodney. 2012. *Heritage: Critical approaches*. London: Routledge.

Harrison, Rodney, Caitlin DeSilvey, Cornelius Holtorf, Sharon Macdonald, Nadia Bartolini, Esther Breithoff, Harald Fredheim, Antony Lyons, Sarah May, Jennie Morgan and Sefryn Penrose. 2020. *Heritage Futures: Comparative approaches to natural and cultural heritage practices*. London: UCL Press.

Harvey, David C. 2015. 'Heritage and scale: Settings, boundaries and relations'. *International Journal of Heritage Studies* 21(6): 577–93.

Harvey, David C. and Jim Perry (eds) 2015. *The Future of Heritage as Climates Change: Loss, adaptation and creativity*. London: Routledge.
Heidegger, Martin. 1977. *Basic Writings*. New York: Harper and Row.
Holley-Kline, Sam and Sabrina Papazian. 2020. 'Heritage trekking: Toward an integrated heritage studies methodology'. *Journal of Field Archaeology* 45(7): 527–41.
Howitt, Richard. 1992. 'Weipa: Industrialisation and Indigenous rights in a remote Australian mining area'. *Geography* 3(77): 223–35.
Ingold, Tim. 1993. 'The temporality of the landscape'. *World Archaeology* 252: 152–74.
Kirsch, Stuart. 2014. *Mining Capitalism: The relationship between corporations and their critics*. Oakland, CA: University of California Press.
Lane, Paul. 2015. 'Primordial conservationists, environmental sustainability, and the rhetoric of pastoralist cultural heritage in East Africa'. In *Heritage Keywords: Rhetoric and redescription in cultural heritage*, edited by Kathryn Lafrenz Samuels and Trinidad Rico, 259–84. Boulder, CO: University of Colorado Press.
Layton, Robert and Peter Ucko (eds) 1999. *The Archaeology and Anthropology of Landscape: Shaping your landscape*. London: Routledge.
Liboiron, Max. 2021. *Pollution is Colonialism*. Durham, NC: Duke University Press.
Luning, Sabine. 2012. 'Corporate social responsibility (CSR) for exploration: Consultants, companies and communities in processes of engagements'. *Resources Policy* 37(2): 205–11.
McGuire, Randall. 1991. 'Building power in the cultural landscape of Broome County, New York, 1880 to 1949'. In *The Archaeology of Inequality*, edited by Robert McGimsey and Robert Paynter, 102–24. Malden, MA: Blackwell.
Moore, Donald S., Jake Kosek and Andand Pandian (eds) (2003). *Race, Nature, and the Politics of Difference*. Chapel Hill, NC: Duke University Press.

Oetelaar, Gerald and D. Joy Oetelaar. 2006. 'People, places, and paths: The Cypress Hills and the Niitsitapi landscape of Southern Alberta'. *Plains Anthropologist* 51(199): 375–97.

Pétursdóttir, Þóra. 2013. 'Concrete matters: Ruins of modernity and the things called heritage'. *Journal of Social Archaeology* 13(1): 31–53.

Pollock, Susan. 2008. 'Archaeology as a means for peace or a source of violence? An introduction'. *Archaeologies: Journal of World Archaeological Congress* 4: 356–67.

Prosper, Lisa. 2007. 'Wherein lies the heritage value? Rethinking heritage value of cultural landscapes from an Aboriginal perspective'. *George Wright Forum* 24(2): 117–24.

Rico, Trinidad. 2008. 'Negative heritage: The place of conflict in world heritage'. *Conservation and Management of Archaeological Sites* 10(4): 344–52.

Robertson, Elizabeth C. 2002. 'Depositional environments and archaeological site formation in the Cypress Hills, southeastern Alberta'. *Géographie physique et Quaternaire* 56(2): 261–77.

Sawyer, Suzana. 2004. *Crude Chronicles: Indigenous politics, multinational oil, and neoliberalism in Ecuador*. Chapel Hill, NC: Duke University Press.

Smith, Laurajane. 2006. *Uses of Heritage*. London: Routledge.

Sørhaug, Christian. 2021. 'Assembling things: Warao crafts, trade and tourists'. *Journal of Material Culture* 26(4): 365–81.

Storm, Anna. 2014. *Post-Industrial Landscape Scars*. New York: Palgrave Macmillan.

Taçon, Paul. S. 1999. 'Identifying ancient sacred landscapes in Australia: From physical to social'. In *Archaeologies of Landscape: Contemporary perspectives*, edited by Wendy Ashmore and A. Bernard Knapp, 33–57. Malden, MA: Blackwell.

Taylor, Ken and Jane Lennon. 2011. 'Cultural landscapes: A bridge between culture and nature?' *International Journal of Heritage Studies* 17(6): 537–54.

Tilley, Christopher. 1994. *A Phenomenology of Landscape: Places, paths and monuments*. Oxford: Berg.

Tilley, Christopher and Kate Cameron-Daum. 2017. *An Anthropology of Landscape: The extraordinary in the ordinary*. London: UCL Press.

Tsing, Anna L. 2003. 'Natural resources and capitalist frontiers'. *Economic and Political Weekly* 38(1): 5100–6.

Tsing, Anna. L. 2005. *Friction: An ethnography of global connection*. Princeton, NJ: Princeton University Press.

Weiss, Lindsay M. 2009. 'Fictive capital and economies of desire: A case study of illegal diamond buying and apartheid landscapes in 19th century southern Africa'. Unpublished PhD thesis, Columbia University, New York.

Weiss, Lindsay M. 2014. 'Informal settlements and urban heritage landscapes in South Africa'. *Journal of Social Archaeology* 14(1): 3–25.

Weizman, Eyal. 2012. *Hollow Land: Israel's architecture of occupation*. New York: Verso Books.

12 On borderlands

María de los Ángeles Picone

Borderlands are inherently ambiguous places. Perhaps the most fascinating and least surprising contradiction about borderlands is that they evoke a loosely defined region ('lands') constituted by a clear demarcation that cuts through them ('border'), even if imaginary. Polities, most recently in the form of the nation-state, have typically constituted the centre of gravity in historical analysis. And polities have boundaries, fringes, liminal regions, borderlands. Scholars have shown for more than a hundred years that this ambiguity tells us a lot about the homogenising efforts of polities. For example, the violence against perceived 'others' might be more evident in border spaces than inland regions of a nation-state. In my own study of nation-making in the border region that is the Patagonian Andes – straddling Chile and Argentina – I have shown how national governments revealed their true colours in their policies towards immigrants, Indigenous people and nature, for the sake of the 'nation'. Here, I reflect on the questions raised by borderlands scholarship and how historians have tried to answer them.

For the first generations of borderlands historians, borderlands meant a place of difference between a growing nation-state, like the United States, and its Indigenous neighbours. In their view, nation-states would eventually eliminate all borderlands. While the historiography has moved past this analysis for nearly a century, its undertones have persisted. The centre–periphery paradigm, for instance, has led many scholars to assume that a frontier space evoked passivity, dependence or backwardness. As Pekka Hämäläinen and Samuel Truett (2011) have discussed, since the 1980s, scholars have deconstructed the binary that simplified power relations in borderlands and examined the plurality they encompass, driving research in all directions, feeding from revisionist narratives and aiming at addressing questions of a more globalised but more bordered world.

Borderlands are not only sites of difference; they are also sites of contact. Exchanges occur among societies that rely on each other, like Mapuche herders selling in Chilean frontier towns cattle the breed in the Argentine plains. In present-day Uruguay, colonial officials used Indigenous knowledge to map the territory. Exchanges, of course, were not deprived from violence. In nineteenth-century Brazil, the *sertão* (backlands), which the Portuguese had deemed 'deserted' during the colonial period, hosted a multilinguistic array of Indigenous groups. They saw their lands as network territories, upending colonial (and then national) ideas about borderlands. States used violence to impose values and norms in their borderlands, but borderlanders also used states to advance their own interests. Hence, analysing borderlands as sites of contact, we are confronted with questions about agency, violence and the environment.

Finally, the study of borderlands helps us de-centre the analysis of how people live, organise, worship, move or trade the way they do. A de-centralised approach enables questions beyond the nation-state. While the centre–periphery paradigm constitutes a useful analytical lens, scholarship on border regions has informed and, in turn, has been informed by questions around fringes, decoloniality and power. Recent scholarship has upended colonial histories that characterised Indigenous roles as subjective to European powers. These analyses have shed light on, for example, Comanche or Mapuche political, social and spatial organisation in North America and South America, respectively, resulting in (still slow-moving) restorative policies. Decentring does not dismiss the nation-state or other organisms as they play out in borderlands. Yet, it enables questions about people's experiences that add dimensions to these experiences sometimes because and sometimes despite national boundaries.

There is a widespread assumption, especially (but not only) among my own historical sources, that borders are given either by nature, God or agreement. Contrary to this belief, borders change and so do the lands around them. In part, they do because polities rise and fall, but also because different people in power invest different meanings to space. Kate Brown examined such shifts in *A Biography of No Place* (2004), where a borderland between Russia and Poland became a Ukrainian heartland in the first half of the twentieth century. The history of borderlands offers a window into other historical processes such as modernisation, nation-making or colonialism. But this history also enables the problematisation of change over time. Did it occur in the same way? With the same interests? Under the same scope? Borderlands might often be presented in the media as unmovable, atemporal fixations. But they are artificial and, thus, historically contingent. The history of border regions, then, facilitates questions on their own temporality in relation to other historical events.

The study of frontier spaces also elicits the question of chronological bookends. The way we organise historical time mostly works because it is a consensus, inherited in most of the world through colonialism. For practical reasons, we have also divided history into chunks of time that more or less dictate methodologies and archival materials. Often, pre-modernists will take paleography courses that modernists need not take. But chronological divides also assume similar frameworks for synchronous events. Borderlands, however, challenge historical analyses construed from political centres. A common framework in the study of nineteenth-century Latin America, for example, is the formation of the nation-state after 1810. At the centre of this process lay the territorial constitution of each country, Mexico, Colombia, Argentina, etc. Yet, scholarship from border regions shows that the formation of the nation-state was later there, or it had other characteristics, or it echoed colonial practices. Agreed chronologies become a little blurrier when focusing on border regions.

The study of borderlands allows us to examine our assumptions about time and space. It deconstructs notions of centre–periphery, it lifts the anchor from polities as centres of analysis and it allows a multifarious analysis of humanity. Borderlands scholarship rests heavily on and fuels other analytical 'turns' in the humanities and social sciences, from gender studies to the spatial turn. In doing so, borderlands offer fertile ground for new questions that add dimensions to historical human experience, as sites of difference and of contact that challenge overarching narratives and chronological divides.

REFERENCES AND RESOURCES

Brown, Kate. 2004. *A Biography of No Place: From ethnic borderland to Soviet heartland*. Cambridge, MA: Harvard University Press.

Hämäläinen, Pekka and Samuel Truett. 2011. 'On borderlands'. *The Journal of American History* 98: 338–61.

Picone, María de los Ángeles. 2025. *Landscaping Patagonia: Spatial history and nation-making in Chile and Argentina*. Chapel Hill, NC: University of North Carolina Press.

13 Discourses and languages

Rachel King

DESCRIPTION AND HISTORIOGRAPHY

Mary Louise Stig Sørensen and John Carman (2009, 6) observed that the 'production of texts' can, in a sense, contribute to making heritage through 'legal texts, official guidelines and indeed academic literature', to name only a few. This view encapsulates something radical in the move from preservationist treatments of heritage to more constructivist ones that set in during the 1980s (see Introduction). Within these earlier frameworks, heritage value was evidenced visually, accessible on its face through the physical endurance of a site, artwork or monument with little in the way of argumentation needed (recalling from the Introduction the thin initial paperwork justifying UNESCO World Heritage sites like the Taj Mahal). The notion that the significance of these assets resides in the *language* associated with them – including the actors, legal instruments and institutions validating that language – as much as aesthetics and visuality is a major methodological step towards understanding heritage value as something that emerges through social action (Harrison 2012, 9). Of course, the words and texts characterising heritage may invoke qualities of timelessness, monumentality and other familiar preservationist tropes, but accepting rhetoric as a site of value creation makes that value more legible and available for analysis in historical and social contexts. That is, for analysis as a *discourse*: a process in which individuals, communities and institutions use official language to authoritatively set the terms of what counts as heritage and what heritage can do.

The early 2000s saw what has been referred to as the 'discursive turn' in critical heritage studies; since then, it can feel like 'discourse' is everywhere in this literature. Discourse as a concept and methodology in heritage research is derived from Michel Foucault's foundational description but has diverged from this as it has been atomised and adapted in heritage scholarship. Following Harrison (2012, 110–11), this adaptation was driven foremost by interdisciplinary critiques of UNESCO's 1972 World Heritage Convention and the many guidelines, heritage designations and forms of authoritative intervention that this has generated. The notion of 'universal' heritage values saw particularly intense scrutiny not only for how this defined universality (i.e. relative to a baseline of Western aesthetics and normative understandings of civilisation), but also for how these concepts authorised particular forms of management and intervention by governments, experts and UNESCO itself (Byrne 1991).

Foucault's formulation of discourse was essential to an analysis of these processes grounded in social relations; there is also a historical component to these frameworks that I argue is equally essential, although it is not often acknowledged explicitly. In this context, discourse refers to the idea that truth and knowledge are not pre-existing in the world but rather complex products of social and historical circumstances (Foucault 1980, 126). Discourses, then, are not inherently universal: they represent the limits of what is accepted as true under particular conditions, including the terms ('the concepts, metaphors, models, analogies' and criteria) for having new knowledge accepted (Kendall and Wickham 2013). Discourse, in this sense, is especially useful for understanding how relationships of power over knowledge emerged and functioned at different places and at different times, although Foucault's characterisations of this power are often vague (Mudimbe 1988, 27). Foucault's (1972, 74, 114–15) methodology for examining discourse seeks to understand how this emerged in a given context: the 'rules of formation' that governed the characteristics of a discourse and allowed it to be accepted as truth, and how these characteristics were replicated and reaffirmed. Among other things, this methodology assumes that the realm of things that *cannot* be said (called the 'non-discursive') is separate from the rules governing what *can* be said (the 'discursive') (May 1993, 31). The non-discursive is a significant, if easy to overlook, part of heritage studies that I return to below.

By the time of the discursive turn in heritage studies, many of the disciplines active in this field had largely shifted from treating heritage as (essentially) less-accurate history to something produced by experts, publics and consumers – a process that could give voice to viewpoints that had long been marginalised in traditional, formal histories and exhibitions (Harrison 2012, 96–112). This amounted to critical recognition that ways of talking about the past could be instrumentalised through various institutions (see Chapter 9), and also that this instrumentalisation was a locus of study (cf. Lafrenz Samuels 2015, 4). Perhaps the pre-eminent example of this perspective lies in a pair of books from 2004 and 2006, in which Laurajane Smith established the notion of a dominant, Western-derived 'Authorised Heritage Discourse' (AHD) that universalises ideas about heritage through instruments like the World Heritage Convention and excludes popular, non-expert understandings.

The first major excursions into more formalised discursive approaches to heritage, and particularly the application of Critical Discourse Analysis (CDA) as a distinct methodology, were well suited to the burgeoning interest in power and governmentality associated with heritage protections. These studies focused on global conventions and legal instruments which responded to and informed one another: for instance, both Australia's 1979 Burra Charter and the 1972 Convention Concerning the Protection of the World Cultural and Natural Heritage (i.e. the World Heritage Convention) reference the 1964 Venice Charter, which in turn references the 1931 Athens Charter for the Restoration of Historic Monuments (Waterton, Smith and Campbell 2006, 344). In principle, CDA is a useful tool for investigating social practice (and especially social wrongs, Fairclough 2010a, 235–9), language and how ideas are disseminated. CDA is multidimensional, moving from examination of the subject texts to how these are consumed in society and finally to how that consumption produces an ideology, all while emphasising the intertextual relationships among multiple source materials (Fairclough 2010b, 94). As such,

CDA could usefully connect the actual words and substance of key texts with the social and conceptual 'work' that those texts do in the world (Waterton, Smith and Campbell 2006, 342) – analyses that supported the establishment of the AHD as a major global phenomenon.

The vast influence of CDA as a method and, to a greater extent, the AHD as a concept may not always be evident in terms of what literature is explicitly referenced in published scholarship (see below and Skrede and Hølleland 2018, 79–80). They are, however, demonstrable where specific terminologies (e.g. 'intangible value', Smith and Campbell 2017), typologies of heritage (Fredheim and Khalaf 2016) and social values (Jones 2017) are recognised as pervasive, mobilising forces. The power dynamics represented by the AHD and its elaborations are also apt for understanding how the Western-style conservation methods promulgated through global heritage institutions found resonance within, for instance, African nations whose domestic legislation retained colonialist ideas about safeguarding the past (Chirikure, Ndoro and Deacon 2018).

Further considerations of discourse have responded to concerns that 'accounts of AHD run the risk of painting a fairly bleak picture, of a consistent and hegemonic system immune to external challenges and change' (Lafrenz Samuels 2015, 4). These include efforts to understand how the experiences of stakeholder communities affect their engagements or frustrations with particular heritage discourses (e.g. 'risk', Rico 2016) and to expand or challenge notions of 'top-down' authority in an increasingly transnational, neoliberalised world (Wang 2019; King forthcoming). Following this line of argument, discourse analysis may not be the most appropriate method for understanding the full range of 'how words mobilize action and effect change' (Lafrenz Samuels 2018, 21) in practice as part of people's lived realities; Kathryn Lafrenz Samuels (2018, 21) has suggested that ethnographic approaches better capture the 'on-the-ground' practices that enact heritage rhetoric. Or, seen differently, ethnographic perspectives – along with those grounded in history and materiality – may complement or correct those relying on a strictly textual or linguistic mode of analysis (Winter 2016). The idea that it may be necessary to amend or pivot away from the original, linguistically based linkage between CDA and the AHD finds support in observations that, by transforming 'processes into entities' (grammatically conflating the AHD as a noun with its verb form) the concept 'masks the very processes that Smith alludes to' by obscuring the actual agency of those shaping the AHD (Skrede and Hølleland 2018, 85–6).

The methods and methodologies that have emerged from these intellectual moves are varied and, for some, 'usefully ambiguous' (Wu and Hou 2015, 37). To attempt a summary of these, we can follow Wu and Hou's (2015, 39) suggestion that they have been united by a focus on the interconnection of social practice and the 'systematic ways of talking about and understanding the world' (i.e. the words and texts used). Attention to the relationship between power and knowledge production is frequently explicit here. Over time, 'text' and 'language' in discourse analysis have been broadened to include sources of knowledge that are not primarily written or spoken – artworks, images, objects and other non-textual data have been increasingly accepted within discursive approaches, each with its own limitations and possibilities (Rose 2006). However, more implicit and less well theorised in these methodologies is the need to understand the specific historical conditions and contexts in which a discourse is produced (this neglect represents one of the main departures from Foucault's methodology). The question of how languages themselves shape the ways in which a discourse is constituted is also often overlooked or under-appreciated (Wu and Hou 2015, 44): how the choice of words in specific languages – with all their shades of meaning and use – play a role in shaping and validating knowledge.

PRAXIS

Investigating heritage as a discourse allows us to work across different timescales and media. Asking how a discourse came to be is a question about the past, while asking how it circulates and is authorised directs us to the present. Appreciating that heritage can be visual and non-visual, textual and non-textual encourages us to consider a wide array of media in our data sources. Therefore, in practice discursive methodologies can require a number of methods, including historical analysis, interviews and participant observation, among others. This means that discursive research programmes can differ quite widely in how they gather and examine data. They can entail tracing specific words, phrases and ideas across a defined set of heritage conventions (Waterton 2010), social media platforms (Bonacchi, Altaweel and Krzyzanska 2018) and management plans or planning documents (Mualam and Alterman 2018); interviewing the individuals and groups involved in validating a heritage concept (Akagawa 2016); or examining how a performance is understood by people deciding whether it represents intangible heritage or folklore (Kirshenblatt-Gimblett 2004). It can also entail asking what people *are not* talking about: the non-discursive elements discussed earlier, such as interviews in which heritage practitioners think some heritage should be kept from public consumption (Zetterström-Sharp 2017).

As I mentioned above, discursive approaches to heritage can ask questions that look to the past (how did a particular idea come to be?), which then entail a particularly historical focus along with the multi-method, multimedia work just outlined. We can see how this unfolds in an example from Lesotho, where I have done much of my research (King 2019). In the early 1990s, historians and bureaucrats in the Ministry of Sports, Tourism, and Culture were seeking international funding to develop the national monument at Thaba Bosiu (where the nation's progenitor established his capital in the early 1800s) as a tourism site. Minutes of relevant meetings, memoranda, briefing documents and letters among key players (all contained in the Lesotho National Archives) show how those working within the country debated the most appropriate form this development should take. There was a consensus that Thaba Bosiu was a sacred, spiritual site, where collective and individual memory was as important to the site's preservation as its stone walling. More so, in fact, as the advisory committee involved argued against rebuilding any damaged structures and in favour of stabilising them while foregrounding the oral and genealogical knowledge associated with the site.

The archives show that the government of Lesotho was able to secure funding and support from the United Nations Development Programme (UNDP) and the German Embassy. The specifics of that support are significant. The UNDP agreed to send three to six archaeological consultants, two cartographers and three museum design consultants. Letters between the consultants, UN representatives and the government's advisory committee show the consultants focusing exclusively on Thaba Bosiu's built architecture, as well as a dispute with the advisory committee when consultants instigated a plan to restore the site's damaged buildings – in direct contravention of the committee's beliefs about where the heritage value of the site lay.

Looking ahead in time, in 2016 UNESCO granted Lesotho nearly USD 25,000 in assistance to inventory the intangible heritage of Thaba Bosiu, including documenting the practices and memories of residents in nine villages surrounding Thaba Bosiu. In short, the 2016 project did what the advisory committee of the 1990s wanted to do but which the UN resources available were not able to supply. The reason for this is (at least partly) discursive. In the time between the Thaba Bosiu development operation and the 2016 project, UNESCO had adopted the 2003 Convention for the Safeguarding of Intangible Heritage, which came into force in 2006 and committed resources to safeguarding 'practices, representations, expressions, knowledge, and skills' – all modes of heritage advocated for in the advisory committee's internal documents. In the 1990s, however, these heritage forms were not an active part of UNESCO's operational framework. Put simply, the advisory committee in Lesotho was speaking the language of what would become the 2003 Convention, but the UN agencies involved with the Thaba Bosiu development did not possess that language – or the ability to turn it into practice – in the 1990s. When intangible heritage and related concepts did enter into the UN's discourse, those agencies came into alignment with the earlier discussion in Lesotho and finally had the necessary tools – the idea of intangible heritage and the management practices this involved – to act on the government's longstanding suggestions. The UN's discourse finally caught up to that of the advisory committee.

Assembling this almost 30-year process involved working with archives from the government of Lesotho, historical and contemporary policy documents from UNESDOC (UNESCO's online archive) and audio-visual recordings from the 2016 project. Unfortunately, because the last members of the advisory committee passed away a few years before I began this research I could not interview them, but that would have provided information about how the interpersonal dynamics within the committee and among the consultants affected the project's progression. The core question informing this work was how those working on behalf of the Lesotho government went about defining heritage and making heritage policy, and so I was interested in the 'systematic ways of talking about' heritage management (Wu and Hou 2015, 39) that pervaded their archives – which led me to discussions of Thaba Bosiu, cultural development and international cultural aid.

TEACHING

How do you say heritage in your language, and what do you think it means? I often begin my (usually linguistically diverse) postgraduate class on heritage methods with this icebreaker. Not only is it interesting but it starts us off by discussing how the words we use and who we use them with shape the way we understand heritage – and then how we act on that understanding. The association between words, knowledge and socialisation is, as we have seen, at the heart of discursive methodology. The exercise just described shows how we can see these elements interacting at the level of the classroom as well as in the higher-up levels that constitute global heritage making.

To that end, and while the place of discourse within heritage studies has emerged through an interest in how ideas about heritage are promulgated from the top down (the AHD), teaching about discourse involves illustrating that discourse does not have a set topography: it does not always come from or go to a specific direction. Preserving the power–knowledge dynamics that Foucault was concerned with is, of course, crucial but this does not automatically mean that discursive methodology *must* seek out top-down power. This is one way in which the notion of discourse has transformed since the AHD was proposed: our understanding of how power and knowledge are constituted has expanded to encompass actors and movements beyond the agencies envisioned as 'up there' in the AHD scheme (Coombe and Weiss 2015; De Cesari 2020). The world's elite heritage institutions – whether multilateral agencies like UNESCO, universal museums or international funding bodies – do not shape heritage discourse in the way they once did, which again highlights the need for discursive approaches situated historically and territorially (Willems 2014).

Teaching students to recognise how published research tracks the ways ideas move and crystallise within a discursive context is a useful way of equipping them to analyse others' scholarship while developing their own. This requires confronting a problem, however: much heritage scholarship does not explicitly state where it engages in discursive analysis and nor does it make clear how the methods involved transform data into knowledge. In part, I suggest that this is a problem of definitions: where research opts to treat heritage as a 'black box' – difficult to define and therefore better examined through the effects it has on the world – the result is a slippery understanding of what, precisely, the relevant data are and how to extract meaning from these. Teaching discursive methodologies in heritage therefore involves identifying where existing comparative research is discursive even where it does not declare itself as such, and what sort of critique that enables. As discussed in the Introduction, tendencies within heritage studies to sidestep consideration of their epistemic journeys have consequences, particularly in how they constrain the use of existing scholarship to train future generations of practitioners.

Earlier, I described another area in which teaching practices can address a gap in current heritage literature: attention to the idiomatic context of discourse. English and French remain the primary languages used by the leading publishing houses and international policymaking bodies responsible for disseminating heritage research – thereby putting a stamp of authority on this research (we can see that this works as part of Fairclough's discursive practice described above). Where research is conducted in other languages and subsequently translated, students can ask of this research the same question they are asked in class: how was heritage spoken about during data collection and what did it mean? As part of developing the capacity to critically read and do heritage research, students can be encouraged to consider how the process of translation worked in real time, how this may have affected the nuances of meaning communicated in a given context and how any linguistic power dynamics may have influenced this (Was a translator involved? How visible are they in the work?). Indigenous scholars have long argued for prioritising retention of Indigenous languages in work purporting to speak for these communities (Tuhiwai Smith 2021, 134); we can interrogate the intellectual work done when these priorities are not shared by publishers or their audiences. This also returns us to a point that Wu and Hou (2015) make: there exist different norms for engaging in heritage discourse and people can be compelled (indirectly or directly) into complying with these norms.

Finally, teaching discursive methodologies is a way of teaching reflexivity about where current and future heritage scholars are already positioned as makers of new knowledge. That is, after all, our job as researchers. As just described, scrutinising the language politics of publishing research is one example of this. Understanding how we participate in shaping ideas about heritage in classrooms, institutions and communities and then developing an ethic of practice based on this is a major part of students' journeys to becoming heritage practitioners, and one that teachers can actively participate in as part of a commitment to methodological rigour.

REFERENCES AND RESOURCES

Akagawa, Natsuko. 2016. 'Rethinking the global heritage discourse – overcoming "East" and "West"?' *International Journal of Heritage Studies* 22: 14–25.

Bonacchi, Chiara, Mark Altaweel and Marta Krzyzanska. 2018. 'The heritage of Brexit: Roles of the past in the construction of political identities through social media'. *Journal of Social Archaeology* 18: 174–92.

Byrne, Denis. 1991. 'Western hegemony in archaeological heritage management'. *History and Archaeology* 5: 269–76.

Chirikure, Shadreck, Webber Ndoro and Janette Deacon. 2018. 'Approaches and trends in African heritage management and conservation'. In *Managing Heritage in Africa: Who cares?*, edited by Webber Ndoro, Shadreck Chirikure and Janette Deacon, 2–21. New York: Routledge.

Coombe, Rosemary J. and Lindsay M. Weiss. 2015. 'Neoliberalism, heritage regimes, and cultural rights'. In *Global Heritage: A reader*, edited by Lynn Meskell, 43–69. Oxford: John Wiley and Sons.

De Cesari, Chiara. 2020. 'Heritage beyond the nation-state? Nongovernmental organizations, changing cultural policies, and the discourse of heritage as development'. *Current Anthropology* 61(1): 30–56.

Fairclough, Norman. 1995. *Critical Discourse Analysis: The critical study of language*. London: Longman.

Fairclough, Norman. 2010a. 'A dialectical-relational approach to Critical Discourse Analysis in social research'. In *Critical Discourse Analysis: The critical study of language*, edited by Norman Fairclough, 230–54. 2nd ed. Harlow: Longman.

Fairclough, Norman. 2010b. 'Critical Discourse Analysis and the marketisation of public discourse: The universities'. In *Critical Discourse Analysis: The critical study of language*, edited by Norman Fairclough, 91–138. 2nd ed. Harlow: Longman.

Fredheim, L. Harald and Manal Khalaf. 2016. 'The significance of values: Heritage value typologies re-examined'. *International Journal of Heritage Studies* 22: 466–81.

Foucault, Michel. 1972. *The Archaeology of Knowledge and the Discourse on Language*. A. M. Sheridan Smith (trans.). New York: Harper & Row.

Foucault, Michel. 1980. *Power/Knowledge: Selected interviews and other writings, 1972–1977*. C. Gordon (ed.); C. Gordon, L. Marshall, J. Mepham and K. Soper (trans.). New York: Pantheon Books.

Harrison, R. 2012. *Heritage: Critical approaches*. London: Routledge.

Jones, S. 2017. 'Wrestling with the social value of heritage: Problems, dilemmas and opportunities'. *Journal of Community Archaeology & Heritage* 4: 21–37.

Kendall, Gavin and Gary Wickham. 2013. *Using Foucault's Methods*. London: Sage.

King, Rachel. 2019. 'How do African states think about cultural property? Rethinking management elites in southern Africa'. *International Journal of Cultural Property* 26: 387–411.

King, Rachel. forthcoming. *The Neoliberalisation of Heritage in Africa*. Cambridge: Cambridge University Press.

Kirshenblatt-Gimblett, Barbara. 2004. 'Intangible heritage as metacultural production'. *Museum International* 56: 52–65.

Lafrenz Samuels, Kathryn. 2015. 'Introduction: Heritage as persuasion'. In *Heritage Keywords: Rhetoric and redescription in cultural heritage*, edited by K. Lafrenz Samuels and Trinidad Rico, 3–28. Boulder, CO: University Press of Colorado.

Lafrenz Samuels, Kathyrn. 2018. *Mobilizing Heritage: Anthropological practice and transnational prospects*. Gainesville, FL: University Press of Florida.

May, Todd. 1993. *Between Genealogy and Epistemology: Psychology, politics, and knowledge in the thought of Michel Foucault*. University Park, PA: Penn State University Press.

Mualam, Nir and Rachelle Alterman. 2018. 'Looking into the "black box" of heritage protection: Analysis of conservation area disputes in London through the eyes of planning inspectors'. *International Journal of Heritage Studies* 24: 599–618.

Mudimbe, V. Y. 1988. *The Invention of Africa: Gnosis, philosophy, and the order of knowledge*. Bloomington, IN: Indiana University Press.

Rico, Trinidad. 2016. *Constructing Destruction: Heritage narratives in the tsunami city*. New York: Routledge.

Rose, Gillian. 2006. *Visual Methodologies: An introduction to the interpretation of visual methods*. London: Sage.

Skrede, Joar and Herdis Hølleland. 2018. 'Uses of heritage and beyond: Heritage Studies viewed through the lens of Critical

Discourse Analysis and Critical Realism'. *Journal of Social Archaeology* 18: 77–96.

Smith, Laurajane. 2004. *Archaeological Theory and the Politics of Cultural Heritage*. Abingdon: Routledge.

Smith, Laurajane. 2006. *The Uses of Heritage*. Abingdon: Routledge.

Smith, Laurajane and Gary Campbell. 2017. 'The tautology of "intangible values" and the misrecognition of intangible cultural heritage'. *Heritage & Society* 10: 26–44.

Smith, Linda T. 2021. *Decolonizing Methodologies: Research and Indigenous peoples*. 3rd ed. London: Zed Books.

Sørensen, Marie L. S. and John Carman. 2009. 'Introduction'. In *Heritage Studies: Methods and approaches*, edited by Marie L. S. Sørensen and John Carman, 3–10. New York: Routledge.

Wang, June. 2019. 'Relational heritage sovereignty: Authorization, territorialization and the making of the Silk Roads'. *Territory, Politics, Governance* 7: 200–16.

Waterton, Emma. 2010. *Politics, Policy and the Discourses of Heritage in Britain*. Basingstoke: Palgrave Macmillan.

Waterton, Emma, Laurajane Smith and Gary Campbell. 2006. 'The utility of discourse analysis to heritage studies: The Burra Charter and social inclusion'. *International Journal of Heritage Studies* 12: 339–55.

Willems, Willem J. H. 2014. 'The future of world heritage and the emergence of transnational heritage regimes'. *Heritage & Society* 7: 105–20.

Winter, Tim. 2016. 'Heritage diplomacy: Entangled materialities of international relations'. *Future Anterior: Journal of Historic Preservation, History, Theory, and Criticism* 13: 17–34.

Wu, Zongjie and Song Hou. 2015. 'Heritage and discourse'. In *The Palgrave Handbook of Contemporary Heritage Research*, edited by Emma Waterton and Steve Watson, 37–51. London: Palgrave Macmillan.

Zetterström-Sharp, Johanna. 2017. '"I cover myself in the blood of Jesus": Born Again heritage making in Sierra Leone'. *Journal of the Royal Anthropological Institute* 23: 486–502.

14 On speaking

Victoria Vargas-Downing

How do we speak about heritage, what languages do we use to name it and what assumptions do we enact in the ways we speak about it? Within the academic context and global heritage management, the language of heritage knowledge dissemination is mainly English, followed by Spanish, French and other European languages.

Whether it is *heritage*, *patrimonio* or *patrimoine*, these terms reproduce assumptions that are entangled with these terminologies, such as patriarchal ways of protecting heritage, Cartesian divisions or linear temporal dimensions. Academics often move within institutional walls and protocols that neutralise other linguistic voices within an academic – mainly English – standard, without much recognition of the ways in which choices and decisions when speaking about heritage are shaped by the languages we use, the ways we speak and the cultures we belong to. How many accents and vocabulary are hidden in this neutralisation? How many other heritages are thus excluded from the canon?

Reducing heritage to only one language, generally a European or Anglo-American way of naming it, limits the ontological approaches to those of the Western hegemonic conception embedded in the chosen language, methodologies and discourses accepted by those conceptions. In choosing a voice, a way of speaking, we reproduce epistemic decisions that are entangled with a cultural background. We are faced with the choice between listening to other voices or perpetuating silences that exclude forms of heritage, the choice between devaluing forms of knowledge and, often, continuing to impose meaning that was set under conditions of violence and dispossession (Muñoz-García et al. 2022).

Then, how many ontological worlds can be opened up by expanding the vocabulary beyond the 'heritage' of the Eurocentric worlds? How many languages and words for heritage have been eradicated, mistranslated or taken away because of the dominance of English or other European languages?

For example, when we think about the future in heritage preservation, Western heritage orientations locate the past behind and the future in front of the eyes, creating a linear future orientation – from the past, in the present, *for* the future. In contrast, for Aymara and Quechua people in the Andes (north of Chile, Perú and Bolivia), the word for the past is *nayrapacha: nayra* are the eyes, while *pacha* means time-space, meaning that the past is a time-space in front of us because we can see it with our eyes; while the future cannot be seen as it is behind us. As a consequence, this concept challenges the linear future orientations of Western heritage conceptions by situating the past in front of us, as something that is possible to see and interact with, and the future is located on our backs, not possible to see but whose burden it is possible to feel (Vargas 2024).

Even the debates that recognise the operation of the Western Authorised Heritage Discourse (AHD) as distinct from Subaltern or Dissident Heritage Discourses (SDHD) are framed as a binary option that resembles similarities to other binary notions such as coloniser/colonised and subject/object. The notion of 'them' as distinct and separate from 'us' reproduces Cartesian categories that aim to control and negotiate knowledge and power, establishing hierarchical superior and inferior categories and values, and reproducing these conceptual separations embedded in Western thought.

Thus, the question of how we speak and in what language we approach heritage is relevant if we do not want to reproduce those systems of oppression because, with different words, new worlds come into existence. For instance, in Aymara language and ontology, the word *jiwasa* is used for a singular and collective person, including the interlocutor. The word *jiwasanaka* means 'we all', a word that is diverse and includes those who are not present. In this sense, instead of an 'us' without 'them', a separation in the English or Spanish terms, the words *jiwasa* and *jiwasanaka* mean 'us with them'. This important distinction limits the relevance of Western conventions and practices to represent Indigenous ways of thinking and being, as well as their utility to drive heritage administration and management.

Overall, speaking and heritage are concepts tied to each other; we learn about heritage in more than written and spoken ways. While the hegemony of English as the academic voice, even in the critical turn, is widely accepted and naturalised, the power relations endorsed by language and institutional structures obscure the fact that heritage manifests in multiple languages beyond academic and institutional worlds. Language is not neutral. Language is complicit in the dispossession, erasure and silencing of other languages. These epistemic decisions can make us complicit in silencing other ways of speaking and thinking. How do we build a field outside these parameters? How do we avoid reproducing these violences? How do we avoid reproducing systems of oppression that erase other worldviews?

The key is to listen to other voices that speak different worlds to us, *voces olvidadas, arrebatadas o silenciadas*, as these voices speak about unrecognised wounds. What has been referred to as *deep listening* can 'help us pull out some threads and insights from the issues in which we feel trapped' (Brearley 2015, 94). This way, *al integrar otras lenguas y voces*, we can attempt '*jiwasa*' – a 'we' in which we are simultaneously interlocutors and producers of knowledge and heritage. Accepting, speaking and listening to other voices on equal terms opens up the field to epistemic and ontological transformation. It is the starting place for speaking not from a place of power but of deep listening: speaking clearly about the struggles, uncertainties and injustices embedded in heritage world-making, and also speaking about how heritage has failed and how it can heal through accountability and vulnerability. After all, '[t]here are modern problems for which there are no modern solutions' (Escobar 2016, 69), and there are heritage problems for which there are no Western words to approach them, but maybe there are non-Western forms of speaking about them.

REFERENCES AND RESOURCES

Brearley, Laura. 2015. 'Deep listening and leadership: An Indigenous model of leadership and community development in Australia'. In *Restorying Indigenous Leadership: Wise practices in community development*, edited by Cora J. Voyageur, Brian Calliou and Laura Brearley. Banff, Alberta: Banff Centre Press.

Escobar, A. 2016. 'Thinking-feeling with the Earth: Territorial struggles and the ontological dimension of the Epistemologies of the South'. *Revista de Antropología Iberoamericana* 11(1): 11–32.

Muñoz-García, Ana Luisa, Andrea Lira and Elisa Loncón. 2022. 'Knowledges from the South: Reflections on writing academically'. *Educational Studies* 58(5–6): 641–56.

Vargas, Victoria. 2024. 'Changing language, changing heritage: The future behind us'. *International Journal of Heritage Studies* 30(1).

15 Practices and performances

Trinidad Rico

DESCRIPTION AND HISTORIOGRAPHY

The 1990s saw an explosion of methods and methodologies for the study of heritage value. Until then, a relatively homogeneous global preservation philosophy and its accompanying methodological approaches had fully embraced scientism and objectivity, allowing select forms of knowledge and expertise to be circulated as a lingua franca. Accordingly, predominant forms of representation and interpretation in the study and management of heritage had been dominated by visual and textual archives and approaches (see Chapter 3). The critical turn that came to challenge the hegemony of these approaches referred to this period as an 'art historical' era for heritage studies. Several concerns converged to bring an end to the exclusivity of this approach. Through the 1990s, a search for diversity in heritage preservation approaches brought to light the extent and effects of Eurocentrism in heritage management strategies across the world. It brought to the surface dimensions of heritage value that had hitherto been marginalised by the widespread promotion of universal doctrinal standards, particularly those stemming from the globalising ideals of the Venice Charter of 1964. The study of heritage has since spread across diverse disciplines and outwards towards the 'peripheries' of a Eurocentric ontology, confronting different research questions and methodological toolsets. One major disciplinary intervention resulting from these encounters was the recognition of heritage value as a value that is intimately attached to practices and performances rather than an intrinsic value rooted in strict material, aesthetic and even historical epistemologies.

Debates originating in the encounter of the field with what was referred to as 'Eastern' and 'non-Western' heritage management strategies offered different worldviews – ontologies – of what constitutes heritage value and its care. Scholars and practitioners examining heritage traditions across Asia, particularly, acknowledged the significance of the *genius loci* (spirit of place), a quality that makes heritage value a constituent part of a distinctive atmosphere (Wei and Aass 1989). This discourse was influenced by the concerns of a humanistic geography in the 1970s that emphasised the importance of human experience and meaning in understanding people's relationship with places and environments. For example, Yi-Fu Tuan's explorations of the 'sense of place' proposed profound attachment to locality as a result of prolonged and sensual experiences (Tuan 1974). It was clear that 'the senses', other than sight, had been generally ignored as a mode of engagement with heritage value in the crafting of a global heritage tradition, as it had been for anthropology (Howes 2023). De-privileging visuality opened the floodgates for challenging not only visual but also historical orientations in heritage value that rely on visual archives. Significantly, it invited the reconsideration of decay as the antithesis to preservation. In Thailand and, later, Laos, studies of local preservation practices highlighted the significance of living religious practices intimately attached to historic landscapes of reuse, decay and rebirth in alignment with Buddhist principles of impermanence (Byrne 1995; Karlström 2005). Decay and destruction as processes of value-making could be contained in authentic practices that aligned with social and spiritual values. Research describing traditional ritual reconstruction practices in the famed Ise Shrine of Japan reinforced the legitimate authority of ritual traditions over global and institutional standards (Adams 1998). The anthropological awakening in heritage and preservation studies had begun.

The rising concern with the role of heritage resources in practices and performances by different stewards and stakeholders disturbed a hegemony of universal heritage value that had frequently severed the relationship between heritage, preservation and living traditions. This critique became formalised through a discussion of an 'Authorised Heritage Discourse' or AHD (Smith 2006) operating globally through institutional efforts such as those of UNESCO. AHD had made anthropocentric experiences of heritage all but invisible despite its emphasis on visuality and the claims to benefit humanity. Efforts to put human experience at the centre of identification and circulation of heritage value required instead a validation of multiple, often conflicting, values contained in heritage that challenged the very idea of a unified 'universal' one. Therefore, intersections with geography, archaeology, folklore, museum studies, public history and anthropology were critical to the recognition and study of practices and performances in diverse contexts. Reparation politics in museums had already recognised different systems of knowledge and claims by non-expert communities, opening the way for ethnographic conservation and curatorial approaches. In this context, 'ethnographic' means 'working with people' in an exchange of knowledge with terms negotiated by both parties and resulting in benefits to both parties (Clavir 2001). Institutional recognition of the rights of communities of interest, which includes their customs, beliefs, social habits, technology, arts, values and institutions, resulted in the development of applied ethnographic approaches. For example, since the late 1990s, the US National Parks Service has promoted the use of applied ethnography in their work (Taplin, Scheld and Low 2002). Likewise, the Getty Conservation Institute encouraged the recognition of a full range of values through their promotion of values-based assessments in heritage conservation and management processes, which includes the use of ethnographic methods to document social values and manage groups of stakeholders (Low 2002). Two decades later, institutions themselves would become the subject of ethnographies that document the ways in which heritage value is contained within the rule of experts and heritage regimes (e.g. Brumann and Berliner 2016; Meskell 2018; Chapter 9, this volume). Archaeology was also a powerful driver in this anthropological turn through its commitment to preserving multivocality and exploring collaborative modes of engagement (Watkins and Ferguson 2005; Castañeda and Matthews 2008; Hollowell and Mortensen 2009).

'The ethnographic' as a way of capturing heritage value recognises the agency of different stewards not just as original authors of resources but, also, as those who maintain – and have a right to maintain – uses and functions of heritage resources. As

Meskell argues, it is an approach that challenges the orthodox notion that archaeology's (and heritage's) subjects are dead, as well as the tendency to see those living agents as passive constituencies for the intellectual mining of preservationists (Meskell 2005). At the turn of the new millennium, the growing significance of practitioners and performers of heritage value was further reflected in the acknowledgement of intangible heritage as a dimension that exists independently of tangible and material qualities of landscapes and things. Through this platform, heritage value as an experience that derives from specific cosmologies could be foregrounded in new ways, including the support for Indigenous curatorial practices (Kreps 2005), oral and auditory transmissions (Hafstein 2018) and religious traditions and spiritual values (Byrne 2014; Rico 2021) in the work of heritage and preservation.

The affective turn in the study and management of heritage value took the project of challenging the exclusivity of scientism in preservation traditions a step further. Joining an interest in the auditory, olfactory and tactile dimensions of value, the affective turn foregrounded the embodied aspects of heritage, engaging with experience, the sensory realm and the affective materialities and atmospheres of heritage landscapes (Tolia-Kelly, Waterton and Watson 2017). It is precisely here, at the margins of the regime of the visual and archival and its longstanding representational traditions, that the limits of heritage methods have been reached, and where personal narrative and alternative archival sources have the most to contribute to the study of heritage value in practices and performances (cf. Waterton and Watson 2015; Chapter 16).

PRAXIS

Months before the COVID-19 pandemic turned entire cities into ghost towns, the exhibition New York Unseen (Yankus 2019) was celebrated in Manhattan for featuring 'perfect' architectural scenes of the city, unspoiled by human interaction – vehicles, people and even animals were artificially removed. Many would argue that an urban landscape is not meant to be experienced as a lifeless architectural model. And yet, this is exactly what the dominant representational tradition in heritage preservation encourages, that is, capturing the perfect archaeological, architectural or ethnographic frame unburdened by unscripted signs of human activity. One need only look at the archive of images attached to each World Heritage List nomination file – predominantly people-less landscapes frozen in time – to realise how pervasive this tendency is (Brusius and Rico 2023). In contrast, consider the way in which the heritage documentary *The Flight of the Condor* (Hafstein and Einarsdóttir 2018) situates historical and contemporary discussions of heritage rights and justice. The authors here curate stills and shots of everyday streetscapes that are a far cry from the sanitised landscapes preferred by UNESCO and other academic settings presiding over the study and discussion of heritage value (Rico 2018). This representational choice results in a narrative that brings an unusual realism to the visuality of heritage as a lived experience: heritage value and voices set in the context of unpaved roads, trash, the noise of traffic and foreign accents, including that of the narrator. In alignment with this commitment, this film depicts the significance of anecdote as a form of knowledge that dominates many narratives of preservation as lived experience.

If only every heritage preservation narrative came accompanied by such a treasure trove of diverse representational media. That they primarily do not is a reflection of the textual and academic orientations that dominate heritage narratives and the expectations of academic productivity. It is also a factor of limitations embedded in the structures of a heritage preservation tradition that is anchored on the idea of a historical archive that gives legitimacy to its work. Beyond the limitations of the text, practices and performances can be directly observed and narrated as they are experienced and embedded in personal and unique ways of seeing. To capture heritage value residing in these phenomenological and affective experiences not only calls for completely different forms of expertise and methodological processes, but also requires a different allocation of time and resources for its capture and translation into heritage languages and platforms. Simply put, documenting human experience happens in a different timeframe to the documentation of façades. For example, Watkins and Ferguson (2005) advise on the seven steps required to work with Indigenous communities:

1. Develop the research design.
2. Undertake background research to learn about people in the region in all aspects past and present.
3. Consult with Indigenous communities in order to reduce or eliminate any adverse effects.
4. Invite appropriate community members to participate, respecting cultural roles and political rights.
5. Identify work products and benefits.
6. Establish rationale for consultation and collaboration.
7. Study ethnography for communication since 'interaction with indigenous peoples, including consultation, is rarely a meeting of equals' (Watkins and Ferguson 2005, 1392).

Those trained in anthropology are familiar with the timeframes involved in this type of ethnographic consulting, although today some of us would argue passionately for a reversal of steps 1 and 6 in order to establish a rationale for consultation and collaboration prior to developing a research design. Nevertheless, the methodological steps above call for longer-term 'situated' study that often involves language training. How feasible is it to transport this method to the study, management and preservation of heritage resources in a field populated by interdisciplinary training and dominated by a sense of urgency? How has this anthropological sensitivity been integrated into the aims and cadences of heritage preservation methodologies? At a practical level, the identification of heritage value according to 'Indigenous' and 'local' cosmologies could be retrofitted into existing mapping and documentation practices through ethnographic mapmaking (Kuznar and Werner 2001; Byrne and Nugent 2004). Cultural resource management strategies used by the US National Parks integrates the interests of different stakeholder groups through their suite of ethnographic methodologies that includes cultural affiliation and lineal descent studies, ethnographic landscape study, ethnographic overview and assessment, ethnohistory, oral and life history, traditional use study and rapid ethnographic assessment (NPS 2022). The latter, a combination of interview, observation, focus group, site walk, mapping and documentary analysis, aims to capture in full the views of various stakeholders whose resources may be affected by the actions of the National Park Service.

The values-based assessment approach championed by the Getty Conservation Institute in their work shares these concerns. Equal parts detailed and vague, it raises two key questions for considering the limitations of all calls for an ethnographic approach. The first question is exactly how consultation happens beyond institutional flowcharts and checklists. It was at the Getty that I first heard Simon Warrack, of the German Apsara Conservation Project, describe a consultation process used for the restoration of the statue of Ta Reach in Angkor Wat, Cambodia (Warrack 2011). Recognising the voice of the spirit as a key stakeholder for the integrity of a religious monument, the conservation team summoned the deity itself, Ta Reach, through a medium in order to seek approval for the proposed intervention. Warrack explains how, upon hearing that his previously restored head would be removed, the medium possessed by Ta Reach cried, only to get up and dance when he was told that his original head would be returned instead. Warrack's approach remains a rare example of a recognition of affectivity in preservation that foregrounds local, and religious, traditions of care and stewardship. While it offers a clear example of the possibilities of such an affect-centred practice, it also leaves us wondering what would happen if Ta Reach had resisted the proposed treatment. To what extent is consultation a process of securing acquiescence to the goals of preservationists?

Herein lies the second important question for the ambitions of a values-based approach. How can any form of ethnographic, affective or phenomenological exchange be attentive to the hierarchies of knowledge in which preservation's scientism dominates over to other, 'non-scientific', ways of knowing and experiencing heritage value? In Mali, Charlotte Joy's ethnographic examination of the preservation of Djenné's mosque captured this clash of realities when 100 years of traditional remudding (*crépissage*) were removed during the Aga Khan Trust for Culture's restoration work in 2006, resulting in riots (Joy 2012). This was partly due to a lack of communication with stakeholders, and partly attributed to the blind institutional belief that a decision-making process could be confined to global preservation standards. While there remains a view that puts scientific or disciplinary value (historical, aesthetic, etc.) above all other forms of authorising practices and performances, the collaborative aspirations of the ethnographic approach can also do more harm than good if done improperly. An attention to heritage ethics in the calls for deliberative heritage preservation approaches helps identify the extent to which experts give shape to value within these rules of engagement (Lafrenz Samuels 2019).

TEACHING

There was a time when calls for a better engagement with practices and performances as ways of making and disseminating heritage value were simply calls for more anthropological presence and training in the field of preservation. After all, the earliest interventions that precipitated the critical turn came by the hands of archaeologists and anthropologists who advocated for heritage value to reside within situated, or localised, knowledge. Traditionally, training programmes in heritage and preservation have not featured a significant presence of ethnographic approaches, especially when located within departments of architecture and planning, as they often do in the US. However, embracing an ethnographic sensibility does not require abandoning one's training. Instead, it should be a process of unlearning the conceptual and practical boundaries that are tacitly part and parcel of the dominant idea of heritage, in order to intentionally, ethically and reflexively apply new ones.

Learning how to study, manage and support practices and performances as loci of heritage value is certainly stepping outside of many preservationists' comfort zones that are, instead, defined by standards, best practices and conventions. What we are stepping into is *ongoing conversations* about archaeology, the past and their perceptions, 'encountering people and places that already have a history of engagement with sites, artifacts, and stories about the past' (Hollowell and Mortensen 2009, 2). The first axiom of teaching and learning heritage value through practices and performances, then, is to recognise the artificial *temporal boundaries* of our intervention on the subject. As Karlström argues, heritage is created in the present, and so its study must begin in the present (Karlström 2009, 17). In fact, material culture theorists argue that preservation itself is an active process of materialisation that makes heritage anything but an empirical reality (Buchli 2002, 14–15) – in other words, the presentness of heritage is a moving target. This recognition, then, demands that we approach the subject of speaking with and speaking for heritage values contextually, in relation to the conditions that allow performances and practices to thrive, as well as our involvement with them.

The second, related, axiom is understanding the artificial spatial boundaries that we create epistemologically in order to turn dynamic practices and performances into discrete episodes and plots. While this is a practical move necessary to allow archiving, translation and often insertion into global heritage narratives, the process of assigning heritage value carries with it a certain stagnation and oversimplification of these scenarios. Practices and their practitioners cannot be easily bound to working categories and, when they do, the privileged position of the researcher or heritage manager over that of the researched becomes even more exacerbated. Consultation and participation are often choreographed at a time and place chosen by the researcher or manager, what sociologists have referred to as a 'third space'. However, the neutrality of this common ground is a myth unless these encounters can take place in common languages shared by expert and non-expert ways of knowing. In fact, the very idea that there is an expert voice and a non-expert voice is problematic. I prefer to call the latter a 'non-disciplinary expert' in recognition of a space that is evidently not neutral – the academic forum, the disciplinary codes – in communications and knowledge exchanges with stakeholders and stewards (Rico 2017).

Thirdly, it is important to question the extent to which heritage value and its stewards are willing participants in the study of heritage and the practices of preservation. All training in ethnographic and other consultation approaches has (or should have) one thing in common: their attention to ethics. In practical terms, this concern has been formalised and enacted to different degrees in different institutions and countries. Perhaps its best known and most longstanding practice comes from the United States, where Institutional Review Boards (colloquially known as IRBs) are predominantly set up within the structures of university research in order to assess the ethics and safety of research studies involving human subjects – aptly called a Human Subjects Protocol (Plattner 2006). Historically, this regulatory approach has stemmed from clinical trials and behavioural studies where the impact of intervention on human subjects has the potential of having adverse side-effects. In ethnographic heritage research, the side-effects to consider might range from the psychological effects of addressing traumatic events in the study of 'negative heritage' to actual endangerment of one's subjects in the documentation of marginalised and oppressed heritage narratives and identities.

The point of obtaining IRB approval, which involves pursuing training as well as submitting a detailed research protocol, is twofold. Pedagogically, it attunes researchers to consider the complex contexts in which our subjects traverse the world in the past, present and future, beyond and through research interventions. In terms of its regulatory power, this training may be the only mechanism for truly confronting the privileged position of the researcher vis-à-vis the researched. For the latter, personal views and experiences become publicly available knowledge controlled and circulated by researchers. The IRB approval needs to be obtained *before* the start of field research activities. This protocol dictates how and when the researcher will obtain informed consent from their subjects, and also defines the strategy for the removal of personally identifiable information (anonymisation) in order to protect their identity when applicable. In countries and institutions where this type of training and certification is not required, rigorous and reflexive training in methods and epistemology can be a pathway to achieving the same goals.

REFERENCES AND RESOURCES

Adams, Cassandra. 1998. 'Japan's Ise Shrine and its thirteen-hundred-year-old reconstruction tradition'. *Journal of Architectural Education* 52(1): 49–60.

Brumann, Christoph and David Berliner (eds) 2016. *World Heritage on the Ground: Ethnographic perspectives*. New York: Berghahn Books.

Brusius, Mirjam and Trinidad Rico. 2023. 'Counter-archives as heritage justice: Photography, invisible labor, and the people inside ruins'. *Journal of Visual Culture* 22(1): 64–92.

Buchli, Victor. 2002. 'Introduction'. In *The Material Culture Reader*, edited by Victor Buchli, 1–22. Oxford: Berg.

Byrne, Denis. 1995. 'Buddhist *stupa* and Thai social practice'. *World Archaeology* 27(2): 266–81.

Byrne, Denis. 2014. *Counterheritage: Critical perspectives on heritage conservation in Asia*. New York: Routledge.

Byrne, Denis and Maria Nugent. 2004. *Mapping Attachment: A spatial approach to Aboriginal post-contact heritage*. Hurstville, NSW: Department of Environment and Conservation (NSW).

Castañeda, Quetzil and Christopher N. Matthews (eds) 2008. *Ethnographic Archaeologies: Reflections on stakeholders and archaeological practices*. Lanham, MD: AltaMira Press.

Clavir, Miriam. 2001. 'The future of ethnographic conservation: A Canadian perspective'. In *Past Practice: Future prospects*, edited by Andrew Oddy and Sandra Smith, 57–60. The British Museum Occasional Paper 145. London: The British Museum.

Graham, Laura R. 2012. 'Problematizing of technologies for documenting intangible culture: Some positive and negative consequences'. In *Intangible Heritage Embodied*, edited by D. Fairchild Ruggles and Helaine Silverman, 185–200. New York: Springer.

Hafstein, Valdimar T. 2018. *Making Intangible Heritage: El Condor Pasa and other stories from UNESCO*. Bloomington, IN: Indiana University Press.

Hafstein, Valdimar T. and Áslaug Einarsdóttir. 2018. *The Flight of the Condor: A letter, a song and the story of intangible cultural heritage*. Film. https://flightofthecondorfilm.com

Hollowell, Julie and Lena Mortensen. 2009. 'Introduction: Ethnographies and archaeologies'. In *Ethnographies and Archaeologies: Heritage and the archaeological past*, edited by Lena Mortensen and Julie Hollowell, 1–17. Gainesville, FL: University Press of Florida.

Howes, David. 2023. *Sensorial Investigations: A history of the senses in anthropology, psychology, and law*. University Park, PA: Penn State University Press.

Joy, Charlotte. 2012. *The Politics of Heritage Management in Mali: From UNESCO to Djenné*. Walnut Creek, CA: Left Coast Press.

Karlström, Anna. 2005. 'Spiritual materiality: Heritage preservation in a Buddhist world?' *Journal of Social Archaeology* 5(3): 338–55.

Karlström, Anna. 2009. *Preserving Impermanence: The Creation of Heritage in Vientiane, Laos*. Studies in Global Archaeology 13. Uppsala: Uppsala University.

Kreps, Christina. F. 2005. 'Indigenous curation as intangible cultural heritage: Thoughts on the relevance of the 2003 UNESCO Convention'. *Theorizing Cultural Heritage* 1(2): 3–8.

Kuznar, Lawrence and Oswald Werner. 2001. 'Ethnographic mapmaking: Part I – principles'. *Field Methods* 13(2): 204–13.

Lafrenz Samuels, Kathryn. 2019. 'Deliberate heritage: Difference and disagreement after Charlottesville'. *The Public Historian* 41(1): 121–32.

Low, Setha M. 2002. 'Anthropological-ethnographic methods for the assessment of cultural values in heritage conservation'. In *Assessing the Values of Cultural Heritage: Research report*, edited by Marta de la Torre, 31–50. Los Angeles, CA: The Getty Conservation Institute.

Meskell, Lynn. 2005. 'Archaeological ethnography: Conversations around Kruger National Park'. *Archaeologies* 1(1): 81–100.

Meskell, Lynn. 2018. *A Future in Ruins: UNESCO, world heritage, and the dream of peace*, Oxford: Oxford University Press.

National Park Service (NPS). 2022. 'Park Ethnography Program'. Accessed 1 January 2023. https://www.nps.gov/ethnography/parks/approaches/index.htm.

Plattner, Stuart. 2006. 'Comment on IRB regulation of ethnographic research'. *American Ethnologist* 33(4): 525–8.

Rico, Trinidad. 2021. *Global Heritage, Religion, and Secularism*. Cambridge: Cambridge University Press.

Rico, Trinidad. 2017. 'Stakeholder in practice: "Us", "them" and the problem of expertise'. In *Archaeologies of 'Us' and 'Them': The ethics and politics of Indigeneity in archaeology and heritage*, edited by Carlotta Hillerdal, Anna Karlström and Carl-Gösta Ojala, 38–52. New York: Routledge.

Rico, Trinidad. 2018. 'The Flight of the Condor, a film by Valdimar Hafstein'. *Cultural Analysis: An Interdisciplinary Forum on Folklore and Popular Culture* 17(1). https://www.ocf.berkeley.edu/~culturalanalysis/volume17/vol17_reviews.html

Smith, Laurajane. 2006. *Uses of Heritage*. London: Routledge.

Taplin, Dana H., Suzanne Scheld and Setha M. Low. 2002. 'Rapid ethnographic assessment in urban parks: A case study of Independence National Historic Park'. *Human Organization* 61(1): 80–93.

Tolia-Kelly, Divya P., Emma Waterton and Steve Watson. 2017. 'Introduction: Heritage, affect and emotion'. In *Heritage, Affect and Emotion: Politics, practices and infrastructures*, edited by Diyya P. Tolia-Kelly, Emma Waterton and Steve Watson, 1–11. Abingdon: Routledge.

Tuan, Yi-Fu. 1974. *Topophilia: A study of environmental perception, attitudes and values*. Englewood Cliffs, NJ: Prentice-Hall.

Warrack, Simon. 2011. 'Learning from local leaders: Working together toward the conservation of living heritage at AngkorWat, Cambodia'. *Change Over Time* 1(1): 34–51.

Waterton, Emma and Watson, Steve. 2015. 'Methods in motion: Affecting heritage research'. In Affective Methodologies: How to develop cultural research strategies for the study of affect?', edited by Britta T. Knudsen and Carsten Stage, 97–118. Basingstoke: Palgrave Macmillan.

Watkins, Joe and T. J. Ferguson. 2005. 'Working with and working for indigenous communities'. In *Handbook of Archaeological Methods*, edited by Herbert D. G. Maschner and Christopher Chippindale, 1372–1406. Lanham, MD: AltaMira Press.

Wei, Chen and Andreas Aass. 1989. 'Heritage conservation: East and West'. *ICOMOS Information* 3: 3–8.

Yankus, Mark. 2019. *New York Unseen*. Exhibition at Clamp Gallery, Manhattan, NY. Accessed 1 January 2023. https://clampart.com/2019/08/new-york-unseen-2/#thumbnails.

16 *Meloro*: on dreaming

Tebogo George Mahashe

It begins with a dream, particularly a dream of a star and the location of a water exoplanet. In most cases such a dream would cause you to visit Moria, where the popular Zion Christian Church (ZCC) is today. The church, by some accounts, is constituted around a fallen meteorite – sedumedi – in the northeastern Limpopo province of South Africa. This beginning is, of course, one of many possible beginnings. It is an example of my attention to dreams that began long before I had this particular significant dream in 2018.

What makes this recent dream of the star significant (so to speak) is that it happens during a moment of intense pressure and stress as I navigated the completion of my PhD narrative MaBareBare, a rumour of a dream (2019). During the course of my research, I had looked at late nineteenth-century photographs as a vehicle for sufficing a longer take of my hometown's early colonial and precolonial setšo (a concept that is related to, but more expansive than, history; see Chapter 14 for discussion of translation practices in heritage studies). In 1897, four sets of my great-grandparents had dared to venture 12,000 kilometres from their secure homes in Vulovedu [Bolobedu] to Berlin, where they engaged in all sorts of activities we do not have space to dig into in this short text. While searching the evangelical missionary archive in Berlin I was constantly frustrated by photography's difficulty with escaping its dominant theories, theories that had been overburdened by the weight and significance of scholars like Susan Sontag. Instead, what had brought me to photography as an archival possibility was the work and practice of photographers and artists like Santu Mofokeng, whose practice in/around/against the colonial photographic archive held the promise of making my story legible. Here, I was interested in surfacing the audacity and curiosity that had facilitated four great-grandparents to explore the colonial metropole in the way in which its colonists were exploring theirs. I had hoped that I could follow up rumours of a group of spies sent by Mudjadji [Modjadji] to draw in the sense of the metropole so that Vhalovedu [Balobedu] could devise a new scheme to continue frustrating or, if a sceptic, to manipulate independence from the colonial project.

After two months spent in the archives, where I found a treasure trove of photographs depicting my home town and my distant ancestors, I could not tell their story because the dominant academic lenses insisted on establishing their presence in this archive and in the colonial metropole as symbols of colonial desire – erasing their own desires or limiting it to what the contemporary Global North scholar could imagine. What I immediately recognised as a possible 'decolonial' context – the persistence of a defiant black Vhalovedu subjectivity – required me to expand or, if I am being honest, waste, precious energy and time on writing my photographic inheritance out of narrow imaginings of nineteenth-century photography as European technological prowess. In this frustration, I took to travel, a methodology I had long practised since Khilovedu [Khelobedu] maintains that knowledge is only possible on the road, for kheredo kha Vhalovedu khe re, the only ailment we cannot cure, is our affinity for the road. You see, Vhalovedu, by their own account, have been travelling, trading ecological security (rain) the whole continent over. In my travels, I encountered a mention of a dream that had been experienced during the voyage and reported to a missionary (Fritz Reuter) who had organised aspects of the voyage in 1897. I would spend some months translating several years of the missionary's diaries without finding the specific dream. The mention of a dream did, in that case, trigger a series of dreams on my part. Or rather, it drew my attention to dreaming as a political action capable of neutralising colonial disciplinary culture. If one could stretch the ideas as a practice capable of enacting the hopes and aims we place alongside decoloniality, this was a demand for taking so-called Indigenous methodologies seriously. The methodology, in this case, being the crafting of a dream instruction capable of bypassing colonial/missionary prescripts. You see, the dream I did find, reported by an unnamed woman, a Mulovedu [Molobedu] who was the widow of the proto-missionary Kgašane Mamatlepa, put missionary Reuter in a tricky situation. It disadvantaged him because she invoked a 'text' whose nature as a dream (*meloro* in Khilovedu) was delivered as an instruction whose imagery may not be subjected to analysis. Presented this way, the dream deprived missionary Reuter of his power to punish – a power that maintained his position as community patriarch. It also privileged Khilovedu protocol in the church, practising ideas of decoloniality as privileging the knowledge practices of the 'Indigenous' people over those of the colonising force. The very idea of a dream as an instruction raised some key technical conditions, including that which dictates that one must dream the dream several times before its implications can be reported as unquestionable cause for some favour or free pass for the person reporting it. More importantly, it established that the only medium for analysing such a dream – which I am increasingly inclined to invoke as *meloro* to avoid confusion with the many ideas invested in the word *dream*, was the act of dreaming itself, not Freudian analysis or logic. *Go etsela boroko* – to journey, which I believe is different to sleeping for rest, was the methodology of comprehending imagery through a Khilovedu lens, what I now appreciate as my intangible heritage. It would drive the epistemic process of knowing in my project.

As I started to practise dreaming – *go etsela boroko bja meloro* – I would grow increasingly confused as one is immediately aware of the multisensory nature of the imagery we reduce to visuals when we wake. What became interesting, in addition to the emphasis on the sonic within the dreamscape, was the role of intuition. As I recently learnt, the body has a sharp capacity for remembering feelings, and when one experiences *meloro*, it is important to focus on what one feels over what one sees. Intuition is the sense that one could focus on what one understood without the undue pressure of the many image-facts constantly fabricated through practices like photography and other media often not in the control of people subjected by colonialism and its practices of marginalisation. What was also interesting was the removal of a concrete document that could be subjected to analysis because in dealing with colonialism, Vhalovedu had concluded that its power lay in the culture's ability to subject concrete documents to scrutiny, resulting in punitive action. So, in my practice of occupying *meloro*, I had learnt that my heritage was one deliberately encased in a medium that would resist colonial agents' access because it demanded a subscription to Khilovedu culture which was, in itself, a process of challenging colonialism.

Considering 'alternative' archives requires a different methodological sensitivity (Mahashe 2019) that de-marginalises forms of knowledge production often dismissed or stigmatised, like rumour, dreaming and walking-about (Mahashe 2020). These among other creative processes allow the researcher to understand and confront the opacity of their subjectivity and subjects of study.

NOTE ON ORTHOGRAPHY

In this publication, I apply Kgotatso Seshayi's experimental Khilovedu orthography, as it is currently being tested by the Bible Society of South Africa in a new translation of the Hebrew Bible into contemporary Khilovedu, to render all Khilovedu [Khelobedu]-language text. At first use of a word in the new orthography, I also provide the popular orthography of the same word in square brackets.

ACKNOWLEDGEMENTS

This work is based on the research supported by the National Institute for the Humanities and Social Science.

REFERENCES AND RESOURCES

Mahashe, George T. 2019. *MaBareBare: A rumour of a dream*. PhD thesis, Michaelis School of Art University of Cape Town, South Africa.

Mahashe, George T. 2020. 'Walking towards a camera obscura/ Marcher vers une chambre obscure'. *Critical African Studies* 12(2): 218–36.

17 Evaluation and publics

David Francis

DESCRIPTION AND HISTORIOGRAPHY

Various intellectual turns in critical heritage studies have led us to the point where it is broadly accepted that publics create heritage value – in our interconnected, globalised era, we recognise how heritage is not just imposed on humanity or citizens but constructed by a wide range of non-'authoritative' constituencies (Wang and Rowlands 2017). In the museums sector, this has aligned to critical reappraisals of the roles of museums in society, including a greater curiosity about how audiences (as stakeholders, consumers and communities of interest) experience heritage curated for them. Implicit in this is a question about knowledge and authority: how do visitors assimilate or shape the knowledge represented in museums and what relationship (if any) does this have to the authoritative knowledge offered by the museum itself (see Chapter 7)? While this and related questions bear on the whole of heritage studies, they have been most thoroughly examined within museum studies where visitor evaluation is treated as a vocational or accountability practice: making sure museums are delivering on their promises to audiences. This then leads us to a further question: what can our methodologies of audience evaluation in museums add to epistemologies of value in heritage studies broadly?

In exploring the history of *evaluation* and its relationship to heritage publics, it is fruitful to emphasise the double meaning of the term. On the one hand, in its instrumentalist sense it refers to the practice of determining the success or failure of a heritage interpretation or programme. On the other, if we follow the Czech museologist Zbyněk Stránský in conceptualising the role of the museum as attributing values to things, then evaluation is related to the study of value (Soares 2016, 5), and therefore aligns with the broader aims of heritage studies. As

Witcomb and Buckley (2013) have highlighted, museum studies and cultural heritage studies have entwined but distinct intellectual trajectories.

The vocational origins of evaluation and heritage publics can be located in the early museum studies of the 1920s and 30s, which used observation of the public's movement through museums to establish some key principles of visitor behaviour, such as the left turn bias or the phenomenon of museum fatigue (Robinson 1928; Melton 1933). These early studies took place in the art museum, but it was in the context of the science museum and the development of interactive exhibits from the 1960s to the 1990s that visitor research in the museum expanded rapidly (Dierking, Ellenbogen and Falk 2004). There was a natural fit between the positivist ethos underlying the discipline and exhibit design underpinned by a constructivist pedagogy that lent itself to evaluate exhibits by trying to measure what visitors learnt from them (Hohenstein and Moussouri 2018). This was coupled with a visitor-focused turn in museology in which the previously sacred role of the object – the traditional receptacle of museum value – was questioned as the best means of delivering the mission of museums (Macdonald 2002; Cameron 2004; see Chapter 7). According to this ethos, heritage interpretation was structured around a series of key messages and the success of an exhibition could be determined by whether visitors retained these ideas beyond the visit.

This focus on measuring what visitors learnt was in turn critiqued for being reductive in its conception of the visitor experience and led to the development of a visitor studies that conceptualised the publics according to identity, affect and well-being (Packer 2008; Smith 2015). An expanded understanding of what was meant by visitor engagement was especially necessary as the evaluation of heritage publics moved beyond the science museum to heritage sites with a complex relationship to national identity, such as the archaeological site of Çatalhöyük (Apaydin 2016), or programmes in which heritage was used a means of narrating one's own journey to medical recovery (Chatterjee and Camic 2015).

Underpinning this shift was a debate about what factors determined a visitor's engagement with a museum or heritage site or programme. Should visitor research focus on what Falk (2016) calls the small 'i' identities – the social group the visitor is with, or the individual mood or motivation on the day to relax or learn about a particular subject? Or were a visit's rhythms and patterns determined by those fixed aspects of identity such as ethnicity, gender and social class (Dawson and Jenson 2011)? The latter position was influenced by the work of Pierre Bourdieu (Bourdieu, Darbel and Schnapper 1991), the highest-profile sociologist to conduct research on heritage publics, whose pan-European study in the 1960s directly linked museum visitor experience to cultural capital inculcated through birth through the family, education and a network of relations.

Central to the state of the evaluation of heritage and its publics now is Witcomb and Buckley's (2013) argument that there has been a growing schism between heritage practitioners and heritage academics. While evaluation has developed a series of tools to determine the big questions at the level of engagement of a visitor site, it has been less successful in engaging with the questions of the critical wing of the discipline of heritage studies. An illustrative example can be seen in Macdonald's (2002) research on the development of an exhibition about food at the Science Museum in London in the early 1990s. Her ethnography drew connections between the exhibition's emphasis on 'consumer choice' and contemporary structural changes driving British museums to be more consumer focused and free-market driven. This analysis was not mirrored in responses collected by the visitor survey, which focused mainly around the confusion of navigating the spaces of the non-linear exhibition itself.

Yet in bringing these two elements of heritage evaluation together, a valuable aporia is created between the critical and the vocational elements of heritage that is crucial to explore. It suggests there is a disconnect between not only the practitioner and the public's conception of heritage value, but also of the academy as well.

PRAXIS

Evaluation needs to adjust to meet the needs of both the academic and the practitioner to deal with the critical demands of this environment. At the same time, we might think of how the innovative series of methods and tools developed for museums and heritage contexts via visitor studies might be pushed into the service of the critical questions asked by heritage research: how do heritage institutions (including, but not limited to, museums) construct narratives through display? How do audiences use these displays to construct narratives about themselves? These entail further questions about enquiring into people's lived experiences at scale (imagine the annual number of visitors in places like the British Museum), and making these meaningful for governmental, financial, managerial and curatorial readers who use the data for various purposes from management to collections care.

Considering exhibition, display or any creative heritage practice as a process suggests a research methodology that pays attention to the stages of production involved – a *chaîne opératoire*. This translated into a particular interview structure in my research on craft making in China's creative economy (Francis and Zhang 2023), although it can apply in other institutional and geographical contexts. I began with an account of when the practitioner first began making the craft; they then talked through and often demonstrated the different stages of making and then this provided the opportunity for a third evaluative moment, which often related to the status of craft makers within China's wider creative economy (Wang 2016).

Gathering insights from visitors to heritage sites presents particular logistical and epistemological challenges. There is a lengthy tradition of visitor research in both observing behaviour and conducting surveys following a visit: namely, the exit interview (Robinson 1928; Melton 1933; Packer 2008). In an evaluation context, interviews are typically short (5–10 minutes in length) to avoid disrupting visitor experiences, to acquire a large number of responses and to reflect the average amount of time visitors spend in a gallery. For my research on 'blockbuster exhibitions' at the British Museum between 2013 and 2015, I wanted to conduct in-depth interviews that would reflect the longer 'dwell times' visitors typically have in a large, heavily invested display (Francis, Slack and Edwards 2012). I recruited visitors beforehand as they queued for exhibition tickets and offered them free entry to the exhibition if they took part in my research. This raised a methodological question about how being cued beforehand might affect visitors' motivation and behaviour in the exhibition itself. Within a free temporary gallery, knowing you were taking part in visitor research might significantly increase your dwell time, which in the British Museum is around three minutes in length. However, the motivation for those visitors who had already intended to visit the British Museum was already high, as they were queuing up and ready to pay for entry. Providing visitors with free entry and a hot drink for the subsequent interview meant visitors were comfortable to give me the time required to talk in depth about their own narrative-making process. In total, 50 visitor groups were interviewed across three exhibitions, consisting of 76 individuals.

The question of how audiences understand heritage through social relationships is significant here: these are social experiences happening among groups of visitors even where people may arrive at a museum or site alone. Within the museum, Leinhardt and Gregg (2002, 159) have shown how when groups talk about a specific object, an idea connected to that object and a thematic interpretation of it, they are building up shared meanings surrounding that object or concept. Group interviews can lead to discussion between the participants that can illuminate an issue and reflect on how meanings are made in the particular kind of social encounters that happen at heritage sites (Roulston 2023).

How researchers interpret meaning from audience behaviour and responses also depends on what questions are asked about – and asked of – audiences. Traditional approaches to visitor tracking have used a positivist methodology: for instance, recording the times and routes a person takes through an exhibit, marking stops on a map, which provides information about which exhibits held people's attention the longest (e.g. Francis, Slack and Edwards 2012). Technologies like wearable cameras and GPS trackers are providing increasingly detailed insights into visitors' dwell time and how they develop strategies for navigating the linear and non-linear components of an exhibition's narrative. Understanding (for example) how visitors used the British Museum's exhibitions to construct narratives about themselves required a more interpretivist methodology, more closely aligned to the ethnographic and practice-based approaches that feature in critical heritage studies (see Introduction and Chapter 15). With this in mind, I asked visitors to recount the experience of the exhibition from entering to exiting. I also provided each visitor with a map of the exhibition and asked them to draw their route, marking up anything that stood out in their minds on the plan and talking me through this: a memorable object, a piece of information they had read, an encounter with another visitor or anything else they recalled. I followed up with questions about visitors' background – how often they went to museums and when their interest in museums and the exhibition's subject matter had first begun. The country of origin, group composition, age range and educational background of the visitor groups was also collected in this portion of the interview.

Decisions about how to handle, manage and otherwise work with data – effectively, how we turn this into evidence – is a crucial methodological element whose specifics are often neglected in more ethnographic heritage studies. These become essential, however, where research needs to be intelligible across sectors and stakeholders. In my work, interviews acted as dialogues in which the findings of my study were co-constructed with my interlocutors and as I read interview transcripts, I searched for threads, tensions and themes (Clandinin and Connelly 2000) oriented by my research questions and the concepts underpinning these. This created themes and subthemes informed by a grounded theory approach, which involved the inductive development of categories related to key narrative elements and the deductive application of these categories to interview data. Key to this was the process of coding, which Corbin and Strauss (2008) describe as a dynamic process of taking raw material to a conceptual level: codes emerged from the data rather than being imposed *a priori* upon it. Processing speech and text data systematically using codes is not always necessary but it does require the researcher to be deliberate and detailed in considering the epistemic throughline from research question to data analysis.

From this approach to the blockbuster exhibition data arose two related conclusions: the central critical issue related to narrative was that those visitors who had the least experience of museums were the ones most likely to both need and accept it, but conversely that those visitors with what Bourdieu would describe as 'high cultural capital' (comfort with and familiarity with spaces like art galleries and museums) were most likely to intellectually and physically reject museum narratives. This has implications for exhibition design, as those exhibitions that provided visitors with more freedom to move and explore were preferred by those visitors with high cultural capital, while those visitors with less experience of museums were more likely to feel lost within these aesthetically led open spaces (Francis 2020).

TEACHING

As a mode of studying heritage publics that are embedded within or at least accountable to particular institutions, evaluation is an epistemology aligned to institutional contexts and constraints. This means that teaching evaluation as a methodology entails teaching students how to gather data within those contexts, which often involve collaborative teamwork. This is in contrast to more common anthropological approaches to heritage studies that envision a researcher as a lone actor. An appropriate pedagogy therefore requires learning to work creatively and critically as part of a collective, and by extension to reflect on how the epistemic journeys involved relate to this coproduction of knowledge. These are features of informal and science education broadly, meaning that a broad, cross-disciplinary community of practice has contributed a suite of theoretical and practical teaching tools related to these principles. As described above, distinguishing between research-led and methods-led evaluation is crucial in differentiating these pedagogies. Tools like team-based inquiry, for instance, offer a cycle of work that begins with clearly defined research questions that clarify the aims and gaps in evaluative strategies (see 'References and resources'). This cyclical nature is also significant: iteration creates a more democratic methodology by continually producing new questions driving the evaluation, which can be determined through consultation with relevant stakeholders. This helps to imbue evaluation with the grassroots ethos advocated by many key figures in critical heritage (Butler 2007).

As well as foregrounding the position of the researcher, it is important to be conscious of the intellectual origins of the methodology as well as its associated pedagogy. This echoes Winter's (2013) call for heritage to move beyond its Euro-American origins and this can be expanded to the evaluation of heritage publics as well. This is particularly important within a non-Euro-American context in which an academic colonialisation can be seen to occur through the importation of heritage theories and frameworks developed in a Euro-American tradition. One approach to this is draw on the work of the Brazilian educator Paulo Freire (1972) and root evaluation within the language of the locale in which the evaluation is being conducted (see Chapters 13 and 14). Within my own work on heritagescapes in China it is important not only that the research methodology is collaboratively created with the participants, but that it also draws on the rich tradition of Chinese social research ranging from Fei Xiaotong to Wang Mingming (Francis and Zhang 2023). This can be taken on both a conceptual framing level – the application of the concept of the term *tianxia* to understand Chinese concepts of the nation-state – but also in terms of the specific methods used such as the ethnological surveys focused on lineage in research on rural village in populations in the 1950s. Teaching students to decolonise their methodologies therefore means relating the coproduction of knowledge in the present to longer, local languages and traditions of knowledge production, which itself requires a related stream of critical inquiry to understand these.

Another key aspect of making heritage evaluation more critical is drawing out the presence of the researcher both in the research design and in the writing up of the results, which presents particular challenges in institutional contexts that students must be aware of early on for ethical and professional reasons. Reflexivity has entered the qualitative lexicon as a way of emphasising the importance of self-awareness, political or cultural consciousness, and ownership of perspective: an exercise for locating the intersection of author, other, text and world, and for penetrating the representational exercise itself (MacBeth 2011, 35).

In my evaluations at the British Museum, acknowledging my professional role as an Interpretation Officer was important both to declare my positionality to my interviewees but also to make sense of my data and write up my results. Initially, the latter was aimed at understanding my professional role: what did we really mean in the museum when we used the term 'narrative' so frequently? Ultimately, though, I felt I could not achieve the critical distance necessary to write about the experience of exhibition-making within the institution; I left the museum as a result. There are professional consequences to doing or not doing this work that must be embedded in how we teach research on heritage publics to students who aim to develop careers within this industry.

REFERENCES AND RESOURCES

Andrews, Charlotte. 2009. 'Heritage ethnography as a specialised craft: Grasping maritime heritage in Bermuda'. In *Heritage Studies: Methods and approaches*, edited by Mary Louise Stig Sørensen and John Carman, 158–81. London: Routledge.

Apaydin, Veysel. 2016. 'Effective or not? Success or failure? Assessing heritage and archaeological education programmes – the case of Çatalhöyük'. *International Journal of Heritage Studies* 22(10): 828–43.

Bal, Mieke. 2012. *Double Exposures: The practice of cultural analysis*. London: Routledge.

Bourdieu, Pierre, Alain Darbel and Dominique Schnapper. 1991. *The Love of Art: European art museums and their public*. Cambridge: Polity Press.

Butler, Beverly. 2007. *Return to Alexandria: An ethnography of cultural heritage revivalism and museum memory*. Walnut Creek, CA: Left Coast Press.

Cameron, Duncan. 2004. 'The museum, a temple or a forum'. In *Reinventing the Museum: Historical and contemporary perspectives on the paradigm shift*, edited by Gail Anderson, 61–73. Walnut Creek, CA: AltaMira.

Chatterjee, Helen J. and Paul M. Camic. 2015. 'The health and well-being potential of museums and art galleries'. *Arts & Health* 7(3): 183–6.

Clandinin, D. Jean and F. Michael Connelly. 2000. *Narrative Inquiry: Experience and story in qualitative research*. San Francisco, CA: Jossey-Bass.

Corbin, Juliet M. and Anselm Strauss. 2008. *Basics of Qualitative Research: Techniques and procedures for developing grounded theory*. 3rd ed. Thousand Oaks, CA: Sage.

Dawson, Emily and Eric Jensen. 2011. 'Towards a contextual turn in visitor studies: Evaluating visitor segmentation and identity-related motivations'. *Visitor Studies* 14(2): 127–40.

Dierking, Lynn D., Kirsten M. Ellenbogen and John H. Falk. 2004. 'Supplement: In principle, in practice: Perspectives on a decade of museum learning research (1994–2004)'. *Science Education* 88(11): S1–S3.

Erll, Astrid. 2020. 'Afterword: Memory worlds in times of Corona'. *Memory Studies* 13(5): 861–74.

Falk, John H. 2016. *Identity and the Museum Visitor Experience*. London: Routledge.

Francis, David, 2020. 'Excavating Freytag's Pyramid: Narrative, identity and the museum visitor experience'. PhD thesis, University College London.

Francis, David and Zhang Lisheng. 2023. 'Crafting authenticity: Two case studies of the material metamorphosis of cultural heritage in China's creative economy'. In *Understanding Authenticity in Chinese Cultural Heritage*, edited by Anke Hein and Christopher J. Foster, 157–70. London: Routledge.

Francis, David, Steve Slack and Claire Edwards. 2012. 'An evaluation of object-centered approaches to interpretation at the British Museum'. In *Museum Gallery Interpretation and Material Culture*, edited by Juliet Fritsch, 153–64. London: Routledge.

Freire, Paulo. 1972. *Cultural Action for Freedom*. Harmondsworth: Penguin.

Hohenstein, Jill and Theano Moussouri. 2018. *Museum Learning: Theory and research as tools for enhancing practice*. London: Routledge.

Leinhardt, Gaea and Sr. Madeleine Gregg. 2002. 'Burning buses, burning crosses: Student teachers see civil rights'. In *Learning Conversations in Museums*, edited by Gaea Leinhardt, Kevin Crowley and Karen Knutson, 139–66. Mahwah, NJ: Lawrence Erlbaum Associates.

MacBeth, Douglas. 2011. 'On reflexivity in qualitative research: Two readings, and a third'. *Qualitative Inquiry* 7(1): 35–68.

Macdonald, Sharon. 2002. *Behind the Scenes at the Science Museum*. Oxford: Berg.

Melton, Arthur W. 1933. 'Some behaviour characteristics of museum visitors'. *Psychological Bulletin* 30(1933): 720–1.

Moussouri, Theano, George Alexopoulos and David Francis. 2019. *Team-Based Inquiry Practitioners' Manual*. London: BGCI.

Nanoscale Informal Science Education Network (NISE Net). nd. Team-Based Inquiry resources. https://www.nisenet.org

Packer, Jan. 2008. 'Beyond learning: Exploring visitors' perceptions of the value and benefits of museum experiences'. *Curator: The Museum Journal* 51(1): 33–54.

Robinson, Edward. 1928. *The Behaviour of the Museum Visitor*. Washington, DC: American Association of Museums.

Roulston, Kathryn. 2023. 'Examining the "inside lives" of research interviews'. In *The Sage Handbook of Qualitative Research*, edited by Norman K. Denzin, Yvonna S. Lincoln, Michael D. Giardina and Gaile Sloan Cannella, 501–20. Los Angeles, CA: Sage.

Smith, Laurajane. 2015. 'Theorizing museum and heritage visiting'. In *The International Handbooks of Museum Studies: Museum theory*, edited by Kylie Message and Andrea Witcomb, 459–84. London: Wiley-Blackwell.

Smith, Laurajane and Gary Campbell. 2015. 'The elephant in the room: Heritage, affect, and emotion'. In *A Companion to Heritage Studies*, edited by William Logan, Máiréad Nic Craith and Ullrich Kockel, 443–60. Oxford: John Wiley and Sons.

Soares, Bruno B. 2016. 'Provoking museology: The geminal thinking of Zbyněk Z. Stránský'. *Museologica Brunesia* 5(17): 5–17.

Van Wynsberghe, Rob and Samia Khan. 2007. 'Redefining case study'. *International Journal of Qualitative Methods* 6(2): 80–94.

Wang, Jing. 2016. 'The makers are coming! China's long tail revolution'. In *Handbook of Cultural and Creative Industries in China*, edited by Michael Keane, 43–63. Northampton, MA: Edward Elgar Publishing.

Wang, Shu-Li and Michael Rowlands. 2017. 'Making and unmaking heritage value in China'. *The Routledge Companion to Cultural Property*, edited by Jane Anderson and Haidy Geismar, 258–76. London: Routledge.

Winter, Tim. 2013. 'Clarifying the critical in critical heritage studies'. *International Journal of Heritage Studies* 19(6): 532–45.

Witcomb, Andrea and Kristal Buckley. 2013. 'Engaging with the future of "critical heritage studies": Looking back in order to look forward'. *International Journal of Heritage Studies* 19(6): 562–78.

18 On digital connection

Colleen Morgan

Digital practice in archaeology and heritage is a vibrant, creative space, ripe for experimentation and play. Using digital tools can help us examine new questions about the past, push our methods of representation, and allow broad access to collections and interpretive material. Yet even as the use of digital tools and workflows becomes ubiquitous and normalised within heritage institutions, it is fraught with unresolved tensions regarding permanence and transparency of processes, and has considerable political and environmental implications. Therefore, when digital tools are used within our practice, the emphasis cannot be on a misperception of longevity and preservation or ease of access or process but must contribute towards building community and increasing the capacity for joy and resistance.

That most things digital will not be preserved is well known to long-time practitioners. The challenges to preservation are intrinsically tied to the charismatic properties of digital media. For example, Richards and colleagues (2021) note the particular creativity of archaeologists in adapting methodologies and approaches with a wide variety of data formats that present difficulties in maintaining standards and encouraging reuse. Closely linked to this is the understanding that there is a lot of failure within digital experimentation, so much so that Shawn Graham (2019) has explored failure as a mode of productive exploration that encourages personal and professional transparency. Further, using digital tools, particularly the proprietary software made by corporations, may be easier at the outset, but can be rendered obsolete, inoperable or simply become too expensive for institutions to support.

As a long-term digital practitioner, I have continually created digital media – websites, digital photos and video, soundscapes, virtual reconstructions and, of course, digitally documented archaeological sites. As such I have created a veritable digital junkyard full of dead media formats, inaccessible files and lost data. In 2007, I joined a team that sought to experiment with a virtual reconstruction of the archaeological site of Çatalhöyük in Second Life. For the next four years, we created multiple interpretations of the past houses and landscape. It pushed us to think in new ways about a site that we excavated for many years. As a result of experiencing the digital reconstruction as an avatar, Ruth Tringham wondered how outsiders might have approached the site, how would you know where to go? By reconstructing ancient architecture, I understood how cramped the interiors may have felt, and wondered if we were excavating the ancient equivalent of basements rather than the primary living space. We also created structures that exist on site, like the dig house and structures that had never existed, such as a digital museum. We held events, created films, made it snow and virtually burned a building following the interpretation put forward by an expert arson investigator. The site now only exists through the media we created, screenshots and the films. Even so, it was absolutely worth the countless hours spent on its creation. Each time I create a digital interpretation, it pushes me to think in new ways about the subject and about my relationship with the subject.

The productive relationship between digital interpretation and knowledge creation in reconstruction is best characterised as *practice-based research*, wherein the process of making digital media directly leads to the transformation of our ideas and positionality (Morgan 2022). I propose that it is not enough to critique existing media, but we must create digital interpretations to understand their affordances. Yet digital technology is deeply implicated in climate change, the use of children to mine materials, and contributes to mental health issues relating to social media and disconnection from communities – therefore, the act of digital creation must weigh the attending costs with the impact of the intervention. Some guidelines regarding the creation of digital media for archaeology and heritage have been devised, in the form of the London Charter (Denard 2012) and the Seville Principles (Bendicho 2013). These ask for transparency, authenticity, sustainability, rigour and accessibility, among other considerations. I argue that these must be accompanied by a consideration of a more critical, activist strategy. The use of digital in heritage and archaeology must prioritise the creation of connections, foment empathy, de-escalate conflict, be antifascist and confront climate change.

With some consideration, the digital can not only fuel our interpretive imaginations, but can support the creation of communities. For example, my OTHER EYES project investigated the creation of virtual reality avatars based on ancient residents of Roman-era York in the United Kingdom. One of the avatars was the so-called 'Ivory Bangle Lady', who is thought to have been of a diverse ethnic origin. Our research team included participation from several members of the European Society of Black and Allied Archaeologists. Together we devised guiding ethical principles through a consensus process for the project that minimised potential harm to project team members and project participants, but also to the avatars or the people the avatars are based on. Through this digital research project, we created a community, one that was based on consensus and connection (Morgan 2022). As such, I encourage digital experimentation, creativity and play in archaeology and heritage, forefronting political, ethical and empathetic practice.

REFERENCES AND RESOURCES

Bendicho, Víctor Manuel López-Menchero. 2013. 'International guidelines for virtual archaeology: The Seville Principles'. In *Good Practice in Archaeological Diagnostics: Non-invasive survey of complex archaeological sites*, edited by Cristina Corsi, Božidar Slapšak and Frank Vermeulen, 269–83. Cham: Springer International Publishing.

Denard, Hugh. 2012. 'A new introduction to the London Charter'. In *Paradata and Transparency in Virtual Heritage*, edited by Anna Bentkowska-Kafel, Hugh Denard and Drew Baker, 57–71. Farnham: Ashgate.

Graham, Shawn. 2019. *Failing Gloriously and Other Essays*. Grand Forks, ND: The Digital Press at the University of North Dakota.

Morgan, Colleen. 2022. 'Current digital archaeology'. *Annual Review of Anthropology* 51(1): 213–31.

Richards, Julian D., Ulf Jakobsson, David Novák, Benjamin Štular and Holly Wright. 2021. 'Digital archiving in archaeology: The state of the art. Introduction'. *Internet Archaeology* 58 (June).

19 Everything considered: training and pedagogy

Rachel King and Trinidad Rico

WHERE? THE FRONTIERS OF HERITAGE STUDIES

It has only been a handful of years since a critical and trans-disciplinary approach to teaching *heritage methods* surfaced as a required course in a handful of heritage and preservation programmes in the US and the UK. But, as we have discussed throughout this handbook, there is a need to strengthen our commitment to epistemology in training. Some of the reasons for this need are related to the trajectory of heritage as a subject of study. As has been discussed by many contributors in this volume, preservationist discourse and practice naturalised specific ways of seeing – identifying, documenting and disseminating – as well as the practices, institutions and value systems through which heritage value was conceptualised. Following constructivist and discursive turns, heritage studies has grappled increasingly with questions of erasure, marginalisation, cultural rights and social justice that revealed value as existing 'underground' – not observable through aesthetics alone.

We should, however, heed archaeologist Denis Byrne's (2007, xii) caution that there are limits to what research 'skill' or 'sensibility' can reveal about the intimacies of these experiences. How we search for the invisible that is also hiding in plain sight – or whether we should search for it at all – has now become one of the major unresolved challenges of this field. If *alterity* hides in plain sight, what is the future of building more robust methods and methodologies for heritage studies?

Other future-facing challenges implicate the ways in which heritage curricula are designed, delivered and marketed. In higher education, heritage is commonly taught at a graduate level (although this is changing) and methods training is often outsourced or aligned to the concerns of other, established disciplines. In this way, historic preservation training as described above aligns with the approaches of architecture and urbanism, curatorial training and museology align with the approaches of art and art history departments, and intangible heritage is served by approaches in anthropology, archaeology and folklore studies. Few heritage programmes are self-reliant in this sense. Moreover, in places like the UK, where graduate heritage programmes are a growth industry, this cross-disciplinarity is often marketed as a unique selling point. The epistemic commitments within particular degree programmes matter because they not only equip students with a suite of embedded analytical frameworks and methodological competencies (which they then take into the job market) but also generate sophisticated dissertation research that then goes on to have its own impacts. Where undergraduate heritage teaching is explicitly coupled with another subject, these epistemic connections are potentially clearer or at least more clearly embedded in curricula. Of equal or greater concern is a tension between market-driven demands for specific degree contents and what is intellectually and ethically supportable within a teaching programme: for instance, desire for experience in conducting participatory research alongside the ethical and practical problematics of carrying this out within the relatively limited scope of undergraduate or master's study, or an even more limited technical training course. Put simply, all programmes of heritage study are not created equally in terms of how they equip students to make new knowledge, and those differences are not always visible from the outside.

At the same time, where heritage is treated as the applied or even economic mode of a particular discipline (history, classics, archaeology), there is a risk of both reifying a set of methods as inherently part of that discipline and also obscuring the intellectual, historical trajectories of heritage in different contexts. By this, we mean that teaching heritage *and* archaeology (for instance, and as we were both taught) yokes the two together through archaeology's preservationist and, latterly, multivocal methods of safeguarding and interpretation. Other methods and intellectual histories involved in managing and engaging with the past that do not fit within this framework are then either omitted or fit less easily within discipline-specific curricula. We can phrase this differently: it was not inevitable that archaeology would make space for heritage in its modes of thinking and practice, and the ways in which this came about implicate particular habits of reasoning, institutions, innovations and exclusions. Our point here is not necessarily that all heritage teaching must strive for an impossible balance between interdisciplinarity and specificity; we are instead arguing that clarity about where methods are situated and their histories within particular fields is essential to the functioning and credentialling of heritage programmes.

The work of research outputs, and peer-reviewed publications in particular, is key in supporting (or not) the teaching of heritage methods. While preservation and conservation-focused teaching resources may maintain a concern with documentation aligned with the standards of different institutions, academic literature on broader heritage studies often obscures methods altogether. We are not the first authors to raise alarm about this trajectory (e.g. Meskell 2015). Drawing from the same concerns with historiography and the legacies of positivist and scientistic methodologies that motivated this volume, Winter (2013, 540) examines the trajectory of the critical turn in heritage studies as it is reflected in key academic journals. He observes two main orientations: on the one hand, a focus on the technical, technological aspects of heritage conservation; and on the other hand, a rising influence of the social sciences and humanities with all their attendant epistemologies, methodologies and methods. These, he points out, circulate in separate fields of academia. The scientific and humanist divide, while maintaining openness to new approaches, results in a study of heritage value that is 'intellectually enclaved, divided by languages and knowledge practices that are, in the end, invariably mutually exclusive'. Although we write a full decade after Winter, the situation has not changed significantly.

How do we reconcile the fragmentation of a field that could yield positive new directions with the ambitions of a field that struggles to take its rightful place in contributing to 'post-western understandings of culture, history and heritage and the socio-political forces that actualise them' (Winter 2013,

532)? We propose that maintaining this breadth is beneficial as long as a more mature and ethical self-awareness of methodological limitations is ingrained in the pedagogical goals of heritage and preservation programmes. One of the biggest ethical transgressions that we see in heritage practice today is the uncritical use of scales and methods that are unsuitable, even damaging, to different preservation tasks. To be more blunt, a 'heritage expert' trained exclusively in materialist approaches (e.g. chemistry) without any anthropological training and familiarity with cultural context should not be making recommendations on or engaging with 'capacity building' targeted at the mobilisation and documentation of social values in heritage. And yet, this type of crossover has been a staple of international and institutional heritage advocacy and work. There are countless more observable contradictions in heritage practice that could be itemised here. This is why every contributor throughout this volume has proposed strengths and weaknesses in the operation of one or more methods. Recognising the effects of operating at different scales and embracing the limits of our own knowledge are the most basic solutions to the epistemological crisis in the field. Knowing the boundaries of expertise is a longstanding ethical imperative (Meskell 2009). In practice, however, the field's 'consultant culture' and the strong influence of fundraising rhetoric that promises grand, rapid safeguarding results has been permeating into academic and pedagogical thinking for far too long. There is practically no space for the acknowledgement of not knowing, or even failing, within that arena of knowledge production. In academic platforms, however, we can and must do better (see Chapter 20).

WHAT NOW?

By the time readers open this handbook, heritage value has already fragmented into what seems like infinite possibilities. The idea of a singular agreed-upon embodiment of heritage value, and a coordinated set of skills and expertise to capture it across geographical and temporal contexts, is simply not realistic. Our hope is that this volume will form one part of a new wave of epistemic journeys that embrace the creativity and cross-disciplinary curiosity that makes heritage such a rich field while also being clear-eyed and self-aware about how, precisely, those journeys unfold. We began this volume by saying that our aim was *research literacy* as well as *research competency*: we want users to feel confident and empowered to ask hard questions of scholarship in order to challenge its intellectual commitments. Setting new expectations for methodological rigour is essential to the health of our field – to encourage innovation and growth, to de-centre epistemologies that no longer serve us and to engage those that have been marginalised.

We also hope that this volume will foster helpful reflections on and new critical engagements with teaching research methods in heritage studies. One way to approach this intellectual work is to ask whether a programme, class or lesson enables a fundamental shift in heritage values and epistemology, or leads to applying potentially innovative methods within longstanding intellectual frameworks. This distinction is essential when considering the effects of, for example, training programmes deployed within global heritage preservation schemes and their abilities to act as venues for epistemic revision. Examples include historical schemes like those promoted by ICCROM, ICOMOS and UNESCO in Africa and Asia which 'trained experts to focus on the Western model of conservation, who on their return to their home countries subsequently strengthened systems that had been propagated under colonial rule' (Ndoro and Wijesuriya 2015, 140). Even where such schemes encourage novel techniques or technologies, their location within established regimes of heritage value inevitably limits the potential for unsettling those regimes. The ability to define heritage epistemologies with precision – in order to critique, revise or dismantle them – is also essential to the health of our field.

Implicit within this last statement is the idea that teaching and practical training can be sites for this sort of work on the foundations of heritage knowledge production. To that end, we encourage students to think critically and literally about their vantage points in studying and doing heritage. The landscape of heritage education – the degree programmes, credentials, skillsets and work experiences – can itself be examined for how it shapes what we know about heritage and how we know it. By this we mean that this landscape looks the way it does because of institutional, historical and relational conceptions of what heritage is worth in the world. We encourage subjecting these realities to the methods and modes of enquiry described in this book (and beyond) as part of what we believe to be a vital shift in heritage studies: embracing heritage pedagogy not only as key to our field's intellectual history and intellectual growth, but also as an arena for subjecting heritage value to further study.

Here, we anticipate a contradiction in our calls for advancing heritage methods and methodologies with a pedagogical aim in mind. While we advocate for respecting the disciplinary boundaries of each approach in recognition of its limitations and contextual considerations, we also encourage readers to critically dismantle the boundaries proposed by this volume. The short interventions that connect, expand and challenge more established approaches in heritage studies – what we have conceived of as boxes to think outside-the-box – are an invitation to chart the future of the field beyond its tried and tested horizons. Diving into the comfort zones of other disciplines that are also engaging with their own critical turn, such as art, history, archival studies, tourism studies, religious studies and visual studies, we anticipate even more productive reconsiderations of exactly what makes an innovative and responsible approach to the study of heritage value in all its expanding possibilities. How these approaches are incorporated into the study of heritage value depends on the extent to which alternative literacies are allowed to flourish (Rico 2021). Some of these remedial conversations are included in this volume, however briefly: for example, the role of dreaming as authoritative 'data' that deserves the same empirical considerations as other forms of data on heritage value. Others are, surprisingly, still absent, or marginal, while they are featured more prominently in adjacent disciplines such as folklore. The senses, in general, have not found a comfortable home in heritage studies, preventing each culture from being approached on its own sensorial terms (Howes 2023; but see Jethro 2020).

Implementing these literacies in training programmes has been difficult for reasons that take us back to a discussion of institutional and disciplinary divides. For example, one of the responses to the universalising World Heritage model has been summarised as a call for more 'anthropological approaches' (e.g. Lafrenz Samuels 2018). How this call is incorporated into many heritage programmes that are not attached to anthropology departments is much more challenging to conceive if heritage studies is to remain a multidisciplinary field. Therefore, the call for 'anthropological approaches' needs to be parsed into its constituent parts in order to be embraced responsibly and sustainably across an extreme diversity of programmes: what exactly is contained in the call for anthropological methods, and how can it be adapted to other disciplinary packages? This type of pedagogical analysis focused on trans-disciplinary implementation needs to be extended to every single 'call' that this volume proposes.

It is difficult to predict, at the time of writing, how the study of heritage will progress, but we already sense the pressure of new paradigms that will, again, steer heritage value into the realms of a scientism and technocracy that erase authorship. On this subject, one additional navigational tool that we offer in this volume is the classic book index. This is a particularly useful instrument of navigation that provides another opportunity to grow our heritage research literacy. As a curatorial and mapping exercise, the selection of index terms to represent much more complex debates and directions is neither neutral nor objective (Brusius 2019). The index terms in this volume were primarily provided by the authors themselves, with some contribution by the editors.

Everything considered, therefore, this volume represents a particular moment in the career of heritage studies as a field. Our hope is that, as the methodological landscape of this field continues to transform, new volumes and programmes built on more diverse and sophisticated theoretical and practical orientations will become necessary – and even essential.

REFERENCES AND RESOURCES

Brusius, Mirjam. 2019. '100 histories of the world in one object: Itineraries, Islam and indices'. *Journal of Material Religion: The Journal of Objects, Art and Belief* (Special Issue: Islam and Vernacularization) 15(2): 243–45.

Byrne, Denis. 2007. *Surface Collection: Archaeological travels in Southeast Asia*. Lanham, MD: AltaMira Press.

Howes, David. 2023. *Sensorial Investigations: A history of senses in anthropology, psychology, and law*. University Park, PA: Penn State University Press.

Jethro, Duane. 2020. *Heritage Formation and the Senses in Post-Apartheid South Africa*. London: Bloomsbury.

Lafrenz Samuels, Kathryn. 2018. *Mobilizing Heritage: Anthropological practice and transnational prospects*. Gainesville, FL: University Press of Florida.

Meskell, Lynn. 2009. 'Introduction: Cosmopolitan heritage ethics'. In *Cosmopolitan Archaeologies*, edited by Lynn Meskell, 1–27. Durham, NC: Duke University Press.

Meskell, Lynn, 2015. 'Introduction: Globalizing heritage'. In *Global Heritage: A reader*, edited by Lynn Meskell, 1–21. Oxford: John Wiley & Sons.

Ndoro, Webber and Gamini Wijesuriya. 2015. 'Heritage management and conservation: From colonization to globalization'. In *Global Heritage: A reader*, edited by Lynn Meskell, 131–49. Oxford: John Wiley & Sons.

Rico, Trinidad. 2021. *Global Heritage, Religion, and Secularism*. Cambridge: Cambridge University Press.

Winter, Tim. 2013. 'Clarifying the critical in critical heritage studies'. *International Journal of Heritage Studies* 19(6): 532–45.

20 On bad (visual) methods

Ömür Harmanşah

There is a fundamentally crucial area of research and knowledge production that connects the visual arts and the humanities yet keeps falling through the cracks of the leaky curricular infrastructures of academia. I would like to call it visual literacy or critical visual studies (or, in a more expanded perspective, critical media). This field is of vital importance as a training ground for our students and the broader public because it gives us an important political and analytical tool to survive the modern world (e.g. Mirzoeff 2011). Yet, it is also a field that is only supported in cross-disciplinary contexts in academia, largely due to the ongoing guardianship of borderlands among conventional disciplines.

By visual literacy, I basically refer to techniques of resistance to the propositions of the literal image, where the image appears documentary in nature and devoid of specific ideological motivations or politics (Elkins 2009). The most basic example is from art history: you look at a landscape painting and treat it as a mere window into the world. The painting itself assumes the role of an observational apparatus despite the deep and politically charged history of landscape representation as a visual convention. Yet, from the definition of the image (still or moving), we often forget that images are brought into existence and crafted with specific agencies and agendas in mind. In the Upper Palaeolithic caves of Europe, hunter-gatherer communities depicted wild and dangerous animals to capture their potency on a material surface that then animated a ritual space. These images of technological mastery and specialised knowledge do not just offer a window into their world of visual experience. When exploring such images, methodologically and pedagogically speaking, I ask my students to investigate what the image *does* (meaning to pay attention to the performance of the image as an agent in the material world), rather than what it *represents*.

Images maintain their visual power that mesmerises us at first sight with the illusion that they are products of an unmediated act of documentation aimed at gathering facts. They purport to be mere residues of what transpired, factual or documentary evidence of archival importance that served as forensic evidence *for the record*! Images take this as far as denying any authorship of the image: aren't the most materially and psychologically powerful images out there apparitions (like apparitions of the Virgin Mary) or religious icons (Pentcheva 2010)? Once you start to dwell on the ideological motivations of the image-maker, that's when the image starts to give away its politics. Therefore, with visual literacy, I am pointing towards an ability or training that allows us to question the genealogy, the politics of the making of the image, and its strategies of visual argumentation.

A good example is looking at a map, a medieval Mappa Mundi or a contemporary cartographic map. In either case, you need the experience and practical knowledge of the convention of representation in each map to read it. While the modern cartographic map removes all traces of temporality from its presentation, the Mappa Mundi preserves temporality through its illustration of itineraries and travel, the literal act of moving across landscapes. This is a basic ability to decipher the map as a representation of the land that it illustrates. Yet this is only halfway towards our goal of critical visual literacy. Critical visual literacy further requires the scepticism that sees maps as part of a colonial act of geographical knowledge production: the making of the map as an apparatus of territorialisation and colonisation, making the land visually knowable as a method of territorial politics. Satellite images and other military technologies of visualisation, such as drone mapping, perform this function as well today. Like other images, maps are never innocent: they are not territories (Turnbull 1994).

Almost a decade ago, I published an article analysing the videos and images published by the Islamic State on global media (Harmanşah 2015). These were choreographed and propagandistic works that featured the deliberate destruction of archaeological sites, museum displays and artefacts of cultural heritage in Iraq, released by the media apparatus of the Islamic State (widely known as Islamic State of Iraq and Syria, or ISIS), a transnational terrorist organisation which was mainly active between 2014 and 2019. The Islamic State's media agency released images and videos targeting sites, monuments and artefacts of cultural heritage with the intention of (a) humiliating the local communities of belonging, (b) recruiting new members to their organisation globally to their base in the Middle East, and (c) undermining the institutions of secular modernity, including museums, libraries, archives and cultural heritage. In my article, I focused mainly on a (now iconic) video posted on YouTube on 26 February 2015, showing the deliberate destruction of ancient sculptures in the Mosul Museum and at the archaeological site of Nineveh in Iraqi Kurdistan. This video was shared across global media in millions.

In my contribution, I critiqued Western academia and global media for their uncritical response to the ISIS videos and imagery. These videos and images disseminated by ISIS's global media apparatus were astonishingly taken for their immediate documentary value to study and determine the nature and scale of ISIS's destruction of archaeological heritage in Iraq. As reports were created for government agencies and funding bodies, the videos and imagery claimed the role of forensic evidence of humanitarian crimes. Western academia failed to understand and respond appropriately to the specific visual media politics. I pointed out that while the Western media characterised ISIS terrorists as iconoclasts or destroyers of images, and characterised ISIS's acts as iconoclasm, I argued to the contrary that ISIS is a *relentless producer of images* that flooded the social media in 2014 and 2015. This political economy of ISIS's image-making was left unexplored.

In the carefully scripted and choreographed videos, we saw an unusual and historically distinct regime of image-making and visualisation of heritage, involving performative spectacles of destruction. These spectacles included historical re-enactments of early Islamic icon breaking. The complex and nuanced politics of global media were unfortunately met with miserably bad methods of visual illiteracy and uncritical reading of imagery. This uncritical reception of ISIS's products of visual media allowed videos and imagery to be disseminated in millions of copies, and directly contributed to ISIS's remarkable success, leading to the growth of their organisation and the eventual suffering of local communities. In cultural heritage studies, the stubborn attachment of heritage organisations and professionals to the conventional paradigm of portraying heritage to be always at risk as a form of participating in the heritage economy is often detrimental to the preservation of heritage.

REFERENCES AND RESOURCES

Elkins, James (ed.) 2009. *Visual Literacy*. New York: Routledge.

Harmanşah, Ömür. 2015. 'ISIS, heritage, and the spectacles of destruction in the global media'. *Near Eastern Archaeology* 78(3): 170–7.

Mirzoeff, Nicholas. 2011. *The Right to Look: A counterhistory of visuality*. Durham, NC: Duke University Press.

Pentcheva, Bissera V. 2010. *The Sensual Icon: Space, ritual and the senses in Byzantium*. University Park, PA: Pennsylvania State University Press.

Turnbull, David. 1994. *Maps are Territories: Science is an atlas*. Chicago, IL: University of Chicago Press.

INDEX

www.ingramcontent.com/pod-product-compliance
Lightning Source LLC
LaVergne TN
LVHW051131260826
846232LV00020B/65